To Barry,
We are thinking
about you + praying
for your speedy recovery.
love,
Colette.

JACK CHARLTON'S
AMERICAN WORLD CUP DIARY

GW00357897

Jack Charlton had a distinguished career as a centre-back with Leeds United and England, with whom he won a World Cup medal at Wembley in 1966, before managing Sheffield Wednesday, Middlesbrough and Newcastle United. He became manager of the Republic of Ireland side in 1986 and has guided them to the most successful era in the history of Irish soccer, taking them to the finals of one European Championship and two World Cups.

Peter Byrne has been a member of *The Irish Times* staff since 1960 and is Ireland's most travelled sports writer. He has covered six Olympic Games, four World Cups and a host of World Championships in all sports. He has been Benson & Hedges Irish Sports Writer of the Year four times.

Billy Stickland has covered all the major sports events of the 1980s and is Ireland's most distinguished sports photographer. USA '94 was his third World Cup. He is the founder of Inpho, Ireland's leading agency for sports photography.

Jack Charlton's AMERICAN World Cup Diary

WITH PETER BYRNE

PHOTOGRAPHS BY BILLY STICKLAND

GILL & MACMILLAN

Published in Ireland by
Gill & Macmillan Ltd
Goldenbridge
Dublin 8
with associated companies throughout the world
Text © Jack Charlton 1994
Photographs © Billy Stickland/Inpho 1994
0 7171 2235 2 (hard cover)
0 7171 2220 4 (paperback)
Design and print origination by Design Image, Dublin
Colour separations by Colour Studio, Dublin
Printed by ColourBooks Ltd, Dublin

A catalogue record is available for this book from the British
Library.

Introduction

This is the story of the Irish team's journey from Italia '90 to USA '94. After the 1990 World Cup, the Republic of Ireland was at last recognised as one of the world's leading football nations.

Failing to qualify for the finals of the European Championships in 1992 was a bit of a setback. We were a bit unlucky but quickly put it behind us and got on with the job of qualifying for America. We had a tough group but eventually got out of it thanks to a lot of good displays, especially away from home, which culminated in that famous night in Windsor Park in November 1993.

Ireland got the toughest group of all in America, the so-called 'Group of Death'. We emerged from it, thanks in particular to a fabulous win over the Italians in our opening match. The second-round loss to Holland in Orlando was disappointing. It ended our World Cup dream and sent us home early. Still, America was a great adventure. As ever, the Irish fans both at home and in the States did the country proud. I know it's a cliché to say that we have the best fans in the world, but it's true nevertheless.

This, then, is the whole story as I saw it. Looking back on it all now, it seems like a long slog, but I wouldn't have missed it for the world.

Jack Charlton, August 1994

I read in my paper this morning that as a result of Italia '90, the Republic of Ireland is now rated the seventh best team in the world, and that the Football Association of Ireland is reputed to have made £1.2 million from its participation in football's biggest carnival.

Those two statistics, in the same story, interest me. The financial health of the FAI is not directly my concern but I should imagine that it's a pleasant change for the Association to be in funds to the extent of seven figures.

The well being of the Ireland squad and its place in the pecking order in international football is, on the other hand, of direct interest to me. And I have to say that it gratified me enormously to discover that the rebuilding programme which Maurice Setters and I started some four years ago is now being recognised internationally.

A lot of people have asked me since coming home from Italy, if I felt our team had fulfilled its full potential in reaching the quarter-finals. Well the answer to that is yes ... and no.

They tell me – and I have no means of confirming it – that the Republic of Ireland is one of the smallest countries to reach the quarter-finals of the competition. In a sense that's a bit misleading for, apart from the Chinese and the Scots perhaps, no country has multiplied more across the world than the Irish.

To that extent we did well to make it past the first phase of the finals at our first attempt. After all, Scotland had never qualified for the second phase – and you know how often they've qualified for the finals.

And yet, I genuinely believe that we could have gone further in the championships. To meet Italy, playing in their own backyard in front of 60,000 noisy, hostile supporters and to have to win the game to stay in the competition was just too much to ask of a team like ours.

It wasn't that the Italians were a particularly brilliant side, but common sense suggested to me and to many others, that they get better as tournaments like the World Cup go on and they were going to be hard to beat at this stage.

Our fellows might play out of their skins, but deep down I suspected that we were not fated to beat them. And unfortunately, from an Irish viewpoint, I was right.

I think it would have been a whole lot different if we had met the Cameroons or Argentina in the quarter-finals. We had the beating of both of those teams, particularly Argentina whom I rated as a modest, predictable side.

With luck then, we might have made it into the last four in Italy. But on balance I think that Irish people in general realised that we did well to have progressed as far as we did.

Even in our most euphoric moments, I was conscious of the fact that the team could have done with strengthening in a couple of positions ... that we needed a couple of better players in key positions to inflict maximum damage on others.

It was at such times that I bemoaned the loss of Tony Galvin from the team which had gone to the European championship finals in Germany two years earlier. For some curious reason, Tony's talent, I felt, was never fully recognised in Ireland.

He was a strong, brave player, who was capable of fulfilling every manager's dream by beating his man and getting to the dead ball line. More than that, he was a diligent worker when chasing back after the ball. Unfortunately, we lost him with a knee injury at a time when I felt he still had so much more to give.

For a time, I thought we had struck it lucky and found a replacement for Galvin within months of his departure. Mark Kelly from Portsmouth was regarded as one of the most talented players of his age group, and I remember one particular match against Poland in which he was little short of superb.

I went home that night thinking that I had solved the problem almost before it had arisen. But I was wrong. Mark Kelly suffered a few bad injuries subsequently, and like so many gifted players before him, he failed to deliver on his promise as a teenager.

Those were some of the reasons why I felt we might have done better in Italy, but by and large I was as happy as everybody else in Ireland that we had made people across the world sit up and take notice of us.

The homecoming to Dublin was one of the experiences of a lifetime. We mightn't have won anything but friends during the 1990 World Cup finals, but when we arrived home, the people turned out in their thousands to meet us.

Unlike us, England had gone to the semi-finals of the competition and were only eliminated on penalties by Germany. Yet, they came back to only a lukewarm reception in London, and that I found remarkable. It was another illustration of the fact that when it comes to football, the expectations of the English are not those of the Irish.

More than anything else, the thing which gave me most pleasure from the entire World Cup adventure was that it made Irish people generally proud of their team. In the sense that I'm employed by the FAI, my first allegiance ought to be to them – and yet, I've never seen it that way.

My primary responsibility, as I see it, is to the Irish people. As long as they're happy with me, the FAI will be happy and I'll be seen to be doing my job properly. I'm sure that they'll have their own particular memories of Italia '90, whether they were in the flesh or as stay-at-home television viewers. But in their heart of hearts they probably shared my suspicion that the system wouldn't permit us to beat Italy.

It's now just over six weeks since the homecoming and already my thoughts are on the 1992 European championship, the finals of which are scheduled to be held in Stockholm in the summer of 1992. In those six weeks, I have mulled over and over again the question of where we go from here.

Some of our critics were unkind enough to call us Dad's Army in Italy. That was a bit over the top. But there is no disputing the fact that before the next World Cup finals in 1994, I will have to rebuild the team, at least in part. The problem now is whether I should use the upcoming European championship as part of that process.

In fact, there is now real doubt in my mind as to how I will meet that situation. Other countries like Italy and Germany tend to be ruthless in that respect and clean out their squad after each World Cup competition. Normally, they keep only the younger players and set out to build a new side around these.

That kind of philosophy is perfectly practical in Italy and Germany where the output of players

Denis Irwin
in action
against
Latvia at
Lansdowne
Road.

from the national championships is phenomenal. But the harsh reality is that we in Ireland just don't have the depth or strength to do things like that.

The Germans or the Italians may be able to throw out a whole team and construct a new one overnight, but my mind goes back to the situation in which I found myself in the run up to the European championship finals in 1988.

Then, in quick succession, I lost the axis of my team as first Mark Lawrenson and then Liam Brady became unavailable. Even to one of the bigger footballing nations, that would have been a huge blow. But to a team like Ireland it was little short of catastrophic.

In the space of six months or so, I realised that I would no longer be able to count on Lawrenson and Brady, and with the heart of the team ripped out, I can assure you that I had some anxious days in the weeks and months preceding the championship finals.

Ironically – and this, perhaps, is a measure of

the situation in which we must operate – I eventually solved the problems in central midfield by switching my two full-backs, Paul McGrath and Ronnie Whelan, into the midfield vacancies in the 1-0 win over Scotland at Hampden Park.

Now, like it or not, I will go for the second option and attempt to bring new players into the team in a situation in which I can surround them with older, experienced professionals.

It is always easier to rebuild your team in that way, over a period of time. Indeed, small countries like Ireland don't really have an option.

The other big bonus is that by keeping the nucleus of the side intact, we can stay competitive in the 1992 European championships. There is a mood of expectancy among our supporters, and as far as I'm concerned, I will do everything in my power to fulfil it. The next two years promise to be very interesting.

20 · November · 1991

Well, interesting that time certainly was. European championship finals next summer! The reassuring bit is that we didn't lose in the preliminaries, and in the opinion of some shrewd judges, we were one of the unluckiest non-qualifiers.

Although I'm scarcely in a position to make a wholly objective judgment, I share those feelings entirely. Without putting a tooth in it, we were the best in our group. But, sadly, I discovered yet again that in football you don't always get what you deserve.

The draw put us in a group involving England,

Poland and Turkey, and judged on what had happened in the World Cup just a couple of months earlier, I reckoned that either England or ourselves would go through. That prediction proved spot on, but unfortunately from our viewpoint, it was Graham Taylor's team which made the cut.

Turkey, I thought, was always likely to prop up the group, and Poland, superb when in the mood but prone to lapses in concentration, didn't look to have the consistency to trouble either England or ourselves.

It all started well enough for us in the home

game with Turkey. Paul McGrath pulled out an hour or so before the game, but three goals from John Aldridge and two more from Niall Quinn and David O'Leary saw us comfortably home.

Then things began to go wrong and, unhappily, we never got back on course again until it was too late. At the end of the qualifying series, many people felt that we blew our chances in the away games against Poland and England, but I don't agree.

The matches which cost us our chance of going to the finals in Sweden were, in fact, the home ones against Poland and England. We dropped points in both and in a tight situation that proved ruinous.

We didn't play particularly well against the Poles; but the thing that annoyed me most about both games was not so much the lack of penetration in the penalty area as the state of the pitch at Lansdowne Road.

On both occasions it was pretty awful, and I felt that we deserved a better effort in preparing the ground by the Irish Rugby Football Union. They own the ground, and while their first responsibility must be to rugby, they get good money from the FAI to present it in a proper condition for international soccer games.

This they failed to do in the autumn of 1990 and I blew my top over it. The channels down the flanks were particularly bad, purely because they had allowed too much rugby to be played on it in the days and weeks preceding our games.

And from our point of view, that was disastrous. We deliver a lot of balls from these channels and we need the ground to be flat and well grassed. On both counts, Lansdowne Road left a lot to be desired when we played Poland and England there.

Unlike the Polish game which ended in a scoreless draw, there were two goals in the England game. But as I judged it, a point apiece was a disappointing return on the day.

I used that game to reintroduce Ronnie Whelan to the team, but it didn't work out as I had hoped. Ronnie had played little or no part in our World Cup programme in Italy, and his sixty-minute appearance against England before I replaced him with Alan McLoughlin was to be his only involvement in the 1992 European championships.

That was an immense loss to the team and a bitter blow to the player. I've had my differences with him, but when Ronnie Whelan was playing well there was none better in all of England. In fact, I reckon that he might have been Player of the Year on two occasions, particularly in the year in which he captained Liverpool to the double.

Alex Ferguson once said of Ronnie Whelan that he did the simple things better than anybody else in the game. That was true, but it wasn't the whole truth. Yes, he liked nothing better than to give or take the short pass, but when a defence needed to be sorted out with a thirty yard ball, he could do that too.

If people were asked to name his best goal for Ireland, they would probably plump for that spectacular effort on the day we played the Soviet Union in the 1988 European championship finals. I liked that one also, but I have vivid memories of another vital goal he scored for us in the World Cup against Northern Ireland at Lansdowne Road in October 1989.

That, if you recall, was a difficult match for us in which we might have gone one or two down in the first quarter. Then Steve Staunton played a long ball which was only partially cleared to Whelan. Others might have been tempted to blast it; but not Ronnie. He coolly picked his spot and threaded it through a cluster of players into the corner of the net. That was an excellent strike – and it was a crucial one.

Unfortunately, he didn't perform to pedigree against England a year later, but in spite of that, we should have won the game. We dominated them early on, but then got caught on the break and found ourselves a goal down when David Platt came steaming in at the far post to put away Lee Dixon's cross.

Had it stayed like that, it would have ranked as one of the great injustices of the sporting year. But, thankfully, we got a little of what we deserved when Tony Cascarino, a replacement for Niall Quinn, got on to the end of a Steve Staunton cross and beat Chris Woods with a clever header.

In that, there was an element of irony, for Graham Taylor, the man who had, only recently, been appointed to succeed Bobby Robson as England's manager, had of course signed Cass for Aston Villa before leaving to take up the England job. And here he was watching his judgment being vindicated in a manner which can only have pained him.

Before the end of that game, Ray Houghton should have wrapped up the extra point for us when he twice got through. As we sat and recounted those chances in the dressing room, I remember saying that I hoped we didn't live to regret them.

Overall, Ray will not have happy memories of our two European championship games against England, for he was to gaffe again in the return match at Wembley. As in Dublin, we found ourselves a goal down when Lee Dixon's shot took a deflection off Stephen Staunton on its way to the net, but then showed real character in

battling back for a fine equaliser by Niall Quinn.

Once again, however, the chances that got away dominated the post-match discussion. John Aldridge's clever flick gave Kevin Sheedy a real chance in the second half, but unfortunately for Sheedy, it fell on his wrong foot.

Then it was Lansdowne all over again as Houghton got through, this time after Cascarino had chested Paul McGrath's cross directly into his path. Only David Seaman stood between Razor and a winner. But this time he pulled his shot past the right-hand post.

The atmosphere at Wembley that night was something special, but as the England players left the ground, I suspect that some of them felt that they had just got out of jail. From where we stood, a 1-1 scoreline was a distortion of what had just taken place on the famous turf.

Our next game in Poland produced one of our best displays away from home; but after leading 3-1 late in the game, we were caught out by two goals and had to settle for a point. For many, that was the game in which we blew our chance of qualification, but I must say that I didn't see it that way.

I remember turning to Maurice Setters after we had gone two goals up and saying, 'You know, we may live to regret this.' My thinking at that point was governed by the fact that England's last qualifying game would take them to Poland, and we needed the Poles to be competitive for that match.

Had we kept that 3-1 lead to the end, it would have meant the end of the road for Poland. But we would still need to beat Turkey in our last game and then depend on the English dropping a point to the Poles to qualify for Sweden. And in that context, I was not disheartened by the 3-3 scoreline in Poznam.

Steve Staunton wins this duel against Latvia at Lansdowne Road.

Let me make it clear that we didn't set out to draw the game nor did we deliberately give away those last two goals. From our viewpoint, both those scores were bad ones to concede, but overall I was not disappointed.

By taking a point from us, it meant that the Poles stayed competitive. And that ensured that Graham Taylor's team would have to work hard for anything they got in their last game. Had we beaten them in Poznam, I'm convinced that the Polish FA would not have spent the money needed to bring back their players from all over Europe, and that would have played into England's hands.

We went to Istanbul for our game against the Turks knowing exactly what we had to do. We had to take both points from the game and then depend on Poland winning in Poznam to squeeze out the English for that place in the finals which we both so desperately needed.

It has to be said that we did our thing in Istanbul perfectly. Although I rated the Turks as the worst of the teams in our group, they are never easy to beat at home, simply because Turkish football fans are so hostile to visiting teams.

Some of the Irish fans who cheered us on that night had harrowing tales to tell afterwards. But down on the pitch, they could have no cause for complaint as we ran the home team ragged early in the second half.

To make matters better, the news I was getting from Poznam was good. They kicked off at the same time, and in the strange manner of these things, the bush telegraph transcended all language difficulties as constant messages were relayed to me sitting in the dugout.

And really, I couldn't have asked for anything better. Not only were we giving the Turks a

lesson, but the Poles had taken an early lead and by all accounts were containing England pretty comfortably.

The last report I got said that there were only ten minutes to go and the English were still trailing. Our players were also aware of what was happening and it made them compete even harder against the unfortunate Turks. If the scores stayed like this, we were through to the finals.

At the end of our game the Turkish manager, Sepp Piontek, came over to congratulate me and said that we were far too strong for his team. He wished me the best of luck in the finals and I said, 'Hold it a minute. We haven't qualified yet.'

He told me that they too had been getting word on the state of play in Poznam and the last he heard was that the Poles were home and dry. And as the two of us walked off the pitch chatting, I couldn't have been happier.

The players had gone to that section of the ground where the Irish fans had congregated. Before going into the tunnel, I turned to give the supporters a wave. It's only then that I notice Mick McCarthy walking towards me and he's almost in tears.

I immediately suspect the worst, and then he tells me. He's just learned from the fans that Gary Lineker has scored a late equaliser for England and the point is enough to send them to Sweden. Bloody hell! I'm stunned. I can't believe we've worked this hard for two long years and now it's all come down to this bitter ending.

Disappointment or no disappointment, I've got to go and get on with my job. I want to be alone with my thoughts, but duty demands that I first go and do my piece with television and radio and then meet the press to answer their questions on the game.

One way or another, it's twenty or twenty-five minutes before I get back to our dressing room, and when I do, I can scarcely believe the evidence of my own eyes. The players, to a man, are sitting there with their heads in their hands and not a solitary word is being spoken. In twenty minutes, nobody has been into the shower and even the back-up people, Mick Byrne and Charlie O'Leary, are going about doing their thing without saying a word.

In all my years I've never known anything like this. Sure, I've seen disappointed players, sat and cursed with the lads who have just seen a year's work wiped out by one bad result. But in almost forty years in the game, I've never witnessed desolation on this scale.

So, I bury my own disappointment and go to work on them. I tell them they can only be proud of their performance and when you perform as well as they have, there can be no room for regret. Sure, they've lost on their qualification bonus, and instead of representing their country in Sweden the following summer, they will have to settle for spectating; but I make the point that they've done themselves and their country proud in this European championship. They haven't lost a game in two years of tough competition, competed like Spartans home and away, and in my book, at least, were the best team in the group.

There would be another day, in another stadium, where the sun would shine again and we would be able to reflect that even though we hadn't qualified for the finals, we had proved ourselves among the best teams in the European championship.

Even as I imparted the message, I sensed that for some people such as Mick McCarthy, that opportunity of playing in another major championship final might never come again. And judged by Mick's reaction when he learned of Lineker's late goal, that thought may have also crossed his mind.

Ever since I accepted the Ireland job, I had come to regard Mick McCarthy as one of my most valuable players, a man you could depend on in fair weather or foul. As a player, he had his limitations, but as a competitor he had no peer in football.

Mick would still be with us for some time, but given his history of injury problems over the years, I felt it was long odds on his being still around if we qualified for the finals of the next World Cup in the United States in the summer of 1994.

That, as I say, made our elimination from the European championship still more painful. But deep down, I was proud of the way we had played. For one thing, it proved that our progress in the 1990 World Cup had been no flash in the pan.

Changes will be necessary over a period of time, but even now I suspect that we will again be a force to be reckoned with in the next World Cup championship. I hope that I am proved right!

7 · December · 1991

*I*t is that time of year again when football becomes even more of a lottery than usual. The draw for the next World Cup is being made in New York, and in the space of a couple of hours our work-load for the next two years comes into focus.

In more private moments, you sit and work out the kind of draw which would suit your team best, but that's pure fantasy. You get all kinds of hunches that you're going to draw such and such a team. But the certainty is that when these whizz kids who organise and supervise the thing get down to business, you'll find yourself a million miles off the mark.

After nearly six years with the Irish team, I find that I'm now a lot more comfortable with these occasions. Obviously, there are countries you would rather not meet in the qualifying stages. But if the worst comes to the worst, we won't shrivel and die. After all, we've been in with some of the best teams around and did OK.

Some managers like to attend the draw in person but I don't see much point in that. It is purely a public relations exercise and the thought of travelling to New York doesn't even cross my mind. Instead, I go to Dublin and watch the thing on television out in the RTE studios in Montrose.

When I arrive somebody asks me if I've brought my atlas, and I answer jokingly that I don't need to – I have the map of Europe imprinted on my mind. What I don't take into account is the fact that the face of eastern Europe has changed dramatically in recent years, and in a matter of hours I will have reason to appreciate the point even more.

In the case of Europe, the element of change in the draw is accentuated by the fact that with the old communist bloc breaking up, there will be thirty-seven countries involved in the programme. And that means that one of the groups will have seven teams instead of the customary six. We can do without that!

As usual on these occasions, there are a lot of side-shows before the real action begins, but it doesn't take too long before the picture begins to take shape. We miss England and instead get Spain as the top-seeded team in our group.

And as the draw progresses, it also becomes clear that we will have to legislate for Denmark in the section. Northern Ireland is the next team to be drawn; gradually, it whittles down to the minnows and it's then that the colour begins to drain from my face.

Against all the odds, we find ourselves in the only seven-country group with Albania and the two new independent republics, Latvia and Lithuania, making up the section. Next morning the headline writers make a splash with offerings like 'A kick in the Baltics for Jack'. But from my point of view, it's far from funny.

Not only do I not know anything about the football teams of Latvia and Lithuania, I don't even know where the bloody places are on the map. It's as much as I can do to pronounce their names. But never mind; in time, I'll become a bit of an expert on the Baltic states.

A journalist asks me if we will play Latvia and Lithuania away on the same trip, and I tell him I don't know. And the reason I give him that answer is that at this point in time, I don't know if, logistically, it would be easier to return from, say, Latvia to Dublin and start back out again for Lithuania. That is a measure of how little I knew

John Aldridge in action against the Spaniards in Seville.

Packie Bonner at the start of the match in Seville.

about the two countries – I'm certain that 98 per cent of the Irish people felt the same way.

It's one thing not knowing where the places are. It's another, more serious matter for a football manager to be unaware of their strengths and weaknesses on the pitch. In this business, most people can put down a marker on a team, for while form can vary from season to season, it is still possible to evaluate teams and players pretty accurately.

The difficulty in this instance was that the Baltic states had been subsumed into the Soviet Union for so long, that it simply wasn't possible for even the most devoted students of form to give them a rating. Traditionally, Soviet sport was so secretive that outsiders were generally unaware of matters like regional representation in national teams. That made the job of assessing our new opponents even more difficult; but I was determined that at the earliest opportunity, I would rectify that situation. Much of the next three or four months would have to be given over to travelling.

I knew only marginally more about Albania. Although they had been part of the European scene at club and international level for some time, surprisingly little was known about them in the West. But what little information there was available suggested that they could be difficult to break down at home.

England had gone to Tirana a couple of years earlier and, amid horror stories of shortages and general deprivation in the city, struggled to beat them. The Albanians' current form is a mystery, but no less than the Baltic sides, they will demand a lot of time and homework.

Northern Ireland was a different kettle of fish. They had been drawn against us in the last World Cup – and I didn't have to remind anyone

that they made it difficult enough for us. The first game in Belfast resulted in a scoreless draw, but we had to endure some moments of acute stress in the return game at Lansdowne, before running out 3-0 winners in the end.

Billy Bingham, the Northern Ireland manager, considered that his rebuilding programme had gone fairly well, but in his heart of hearts – and they don't come more astute than Billy – I think he realised he was one or two players short of having a good team.

That is why I said immediately after the draw that I felt that the two qualifying places lay between Spain, Denmark and ourselves – and immediately landed myself in hot water with my many friends north of the border.

Nothing would give me greater pleasure than to see the two Ireland teams going through to the finals, but I genuinely believe Billy's team to be suspect in a couple of areas. And in my dealings with the press, I've always believed that an honest question deserves an honest answer.

Now Spain and Denmark were different. Neither had made much of an impact in the last World Cup, but they were beginning to get their act together again and, with decent luck, would be a force in international football once more.

The Spaniards had always been among the heavyweights, a team which could beat anybody when playing at home. For years they played their bigger home games in Madrid, but more recently they had adopted Seville as their capital for football – with disastrous results for all visiting teams.

The crowds turning up for games in Seville were particularly partisan! The players seemed to respond in the most positive manner to that support, and the result was that very few teams venturing into that setting for the first time left with a draw, let alone a win.

We had gone there in November 1988, shortly after the European championships in Germany, and lost 2-0. In fairness though, I always felt that the scoreline was a bit misleading. For one reason or another, we were without more than half our team and ended up playing Kevin Moran in midfield. That was real desperation stakes, and it showed in our performance.

Against that, however, the Spaniards were regarded among the worst travellers in football. For all their resources – and remember they operate from the base of one of the stronger league championships in Europe – they never seemed to deliver on their pedigree away from home.

All that, I hasten to add, was in the past. More recently, they have been attaining greater consistency in their performances outside Spain, and I know that other managers are now beginning to view them in a different light.

Ever since Sepp Piontek arrived from Germany and gave them a new sense of self-belief, Denmark have been one of Europe's better teams and, like Spain, I reckon they are on the way back.

They benefit from the fact that many of their players are based in other countries, and when they get them all together, it gives the side an interesting balance. They have a couple of outstanding defenders, and in Brian Laudrup they can justly claim to possess probably the best striker in Europe.

Laudrup on the burst is one of the most exciting spectacles in football, and already I am figuring out in the mind's eye just how we will cope with him. One thing is for certain: given

half a chance, he is capable of wrecking any defence irrespective of how carefully it is constructed.

That then is the grouping in which we find ourselves, and I must say that my initial reaction is one of disappointment. Strange as it may seem, I would like the section to be more competitive – I would welcome the inclusion of a fourth team with the ability to go and take points off the big three.

The way I view it, there is too much of a gap between the first bunch, comprising Spain, Denmark and ourselves, and the rest. It seems to me at this stage that few if any of the smaller teams will be capable of taking points from the favourites.

Time may prove me wrong on that count, but from where I stand, it looks like condensing into a situation in which qualification will depend on the three best teams taking points off each other.

Contrast that, for example, with the situation in England's group. In fact, the only team already out of it in that particular grouping is San Marino. Like myself, Graham Taylor will be examining the different options open to him. But in his case, I feel there are safety nets available to him even if they come unstuck in their early games.

That kind of escape route will not be on offer in Group Three. If we are beaten at home by either Spain or the Danes, it threatens to be expensive – and the same threat, of course, hangs over them.

There is always the possibility that the journeys to Albania and the Baltics will prove more treacherous than is generally accepted. In that case it will be interesting.

At the start of the Northern Ireland match at Lansdowne Road, a minute's silence was observed for victims of the Northern Troubles.

 Niall Quinn and Gerry Taggart tussle for the ball at Lansdowne Road.

John Aldridge challenges the Albanian goalkeeper in Tirana.

 Once again, Aldo was in the thick of everything against the Lithuanians.

 Paul McGrath goes highest against Lithuania.

Steve Staunton's name was obviously not too familiar to the scoreboard operator in Vilnius.

23 · January · 1992

I wasn't too long into my job with the FAI before I realised that there was more to do than choosing and preparing squads for games. I soon discovered that the dates of these fixtures, and the problems in playing away or at home at different stages of the season, also had a very big bearing in determining whether you achieved the desired results.

It was the preliminaries of the 1988 European championships which gave me my first insight into the intricacies of this particular aspect of management. That was a real learning experience, and by the time I was required to repeat that assignment for the qualifying rounds of the World Cup two years later, I was better prepared to cope with the wheeling and dealing bit.

My experience on those two missions was that you're never going to get everything you want, that you're never going to return to base with the perfect set of dates locked away in the briefcase.

Almost without exception, it comes down to an exercise in compromise. The important thing is not to have to yield on the games that matter most. But this, as I quickly found out, was easier said than done.

By the time I arrived in Copenhagen for the meeting which would sort out the dates and the venues for Group Three fixtures, I was pretty clear on what I wanted. But I was also grimly aware that this was going to be a more tricky job than either of those I had handled previously.

For one thing, there were more games than normal to be played. Because of the fact that we ended up in the only seven-country section in the European part of the draw, it meant that we were going to have to play twelve games in the space of eighteen months.

On the face of it, that may not sound unreasonable, but when you get down to the details, the difficulties involved are all too apparent. Obviously nobody wants to play out of season, but even in season there is the huge problem of fitting twelve competitive internationals into a club schedule which is already top heavy.

And, of course, there are always additional considerations. We, for example, cannot have the use of Lansdowne Road between the last week in October and the last week in March, while the Baltic teams, with grounds that are frozen over for a number of months, are likewise restricted in their choice of dates.

Given these parameters, the talking in Copenhagen was always going to be tough; but as I said earlier, I knew exactly what my requirements were. Firstly, I needed the psychological boost of a good start, and with that in mind, I set out to get our two easiest home games arranged for the start of our programme.

Albania and Latvia fitted the description of teams we could beat with some ease in Dublin, which would give us four points and a place at the top of the table before we ventured abroad and applied ourselves to the challenge of proving that we are, indeed, the best team in the group.

Nothing has happened in the last six weeks to shake my conviction that the two qualifying places rest between Spain, Denmark and ourselves. I plan to look at the Danes at the earliest opportunity, but I have just returned from watching Spain in a friendly against

Portugal in Lisbon, and I am suitably impressed.

It follows, then, that I regard our games in Spain and Denmark as the most difficult in our entire schedule, and I resolve that in so far as it is possible, we will play them at the start of next season. Whether the Danes or the Spaniards agree is another thing. But I want these two matches out of the way by Christmas.

My reasons are twofold. Players involved in English club football will still be fresh at that stage, whereas if we wait until the second half of the season, it may well emerge that they are beginning to feel the pinch. Clubs are demanding more and more from their players, and since they pay the wages, there is nothing that we can do about that situation.

But if my little scheme works, it will ensure that we will get the best out of the lads at a time when we need it most. The variable that we simply cannot legislate for is injury. The prospect of going into either match without key players is already beginning to haunt me.

The other big plus for me in getting early season fixtures in Spain and Denmark is that the qualifying process will still be only in its infancy at that stage. It will not, hopefully, generate a win or bust attitude on the part of either the Spaniards or the Danes, and that will obviously be to our advantage.

The last thing I want is to have to go to either Seville or Copenhagen in our last game looking for a draw, or worse still, a win to qualify. I'm getting too old for tension like that.

I soon find out that the Spaniards are ready to facilitate us in every way, even to the extent of coming to Dublin for the second last game in the qualifying series in October 1993 at a stage, hopefully, when we will have done all the hard work in booking that transatlantic flight for the World Cup finals.

Denmark, too, are co-operative about playing us in Copenhagen in October 1992, but in this instance, there is a sting in the tail. I want them back in Dublin in the last week of May '93, whereas they are adamant that the game should go on four weeks earlier.

To some it may smack of nit-picking, and I'm sure many people will ask what real difference a mere month will make. Well, my answer to that is a lot, a hell of a lot of difference if it comes down in the end to a head-to-head between the Danes and ourselves.

As I've mentioned before, the FAI has the use of Lansdowne from the last week in March, but bitter experience has taught that the pitch can be appalling for a March game there, and only marginally better for one in April. The international rugby programme may be over at that stage, but they tend to play a lot of club rugby there in April. And with the ruts and bumps drying out and little or no grass to kill the pace on the ball, that creates a lot of problems for soccer.

The Danish delegation was scarcely aware of that situation; but rightly or wrongly, they insisted on playing in Dublin on 28 April. Eventually I gave in, but even now I suspect that it is a decision we might yet live to regret.

That was a minus as far as I was concerned. So too were the arrangements for the away games in Albania, Latvia and Lithuania at the end of the 1992/93 season. Ideally, I wanted to take in those three fixtures on the same tour, but it soon became clear that this was a non-starter.

The Albanians insisted that they could play us in Tirana only at the end of May, when they would have all their better players back from Europe; whereas the two

Baltic teams insisted that they had to have dates well into June.

So a programme which could have been disposed of in nine or ten days would now occupy our attention for three weeks. And that was an imposition on the players which I resented.

By that stage they would have been on the job, either in club or international football, for eleven months. And with the Lithuanian game scheduled for Vilnius on 16 June, it would mean a break of less than four weeks for many before they were back in pre-season training.

The critics would have you believe that ours is the 1990 World Cup team all over again, but that's not true. Gradually, I've been grooming new, younger players to come into the side, and now I'm looking to two of them, Denis Irwin and Roy Keane, to do an important job for me.

Chris Morris has been one of my best and most dependable players since I began to rebuild the Ireland side in the second half of the eighties. He is still an extremely useful player to have in the squad, but more and more, I'm impressed with Irwin's performances at full-back.

Ever since his Oldham days I've liked this player, and his move to Manchester United has given him the chance to express his talent on a bigger stage. He's quick and he crosses the ball well, and as he's shown on occasions for Manchester United, he's capable of scoring some important goals.

The other newcomer, Roy Keane, is also a Cork man. But unlike Denis, a shy man who gets on with his job quietly and efficiently, Roy is seldom out of the news. And given his prodigious talent, that is not altogether surprising.

I said earlier that I felt we could have been stronger in one or two positions for the 1990 finals in Italy, and one of the people we could

have done with out there was Roy Keane. Unfortunately, he was still only in youth football at the time and it would be another two or three years before he would graduate fully into senior competition.

So many superlatives have been used to describe the lad, that it's difficult to know where to start. He's strong; he reads the game well for one so young; and even at 21, he is a manager's dream inasmuch as he can slot into three or four different roles.

But the thing I admire most about him is his engine. Even on the heaviest of grounds, he looks to be capable of running all day. That's a priceless asset in any youngster, and when you marry that with the superb skills Roy has, you come up with a very special player. We've been aware of him for some years – in fact, I think Maurice Setters had a part in his going to England as a boy.

The fact that Ireland exports so many young players to England upsets people, but I for one see nothing wrong with it. It would be nice, of course, if we had a major championship in Ireland and we could develop our youngsters here at home. Unfortunately, that is not the case and so we must work within the existing system. England is the academy of our schoolboy players, and while some may view it differently, I make no apology for encouraging lads to go there.

I was reasonably satisfied with the dates for the two Northern Ireland games, 31 March 1993 in Dublin and 17 November in Belfast. The March date at Lansdowne would, as ever, be tricky, but I figured we could cope against the Northern Irish even on a bad playing surface.

I know I've ruffled a few feathers north of the border by predicting that Billy Bingham's team will not qualify for the finals, for the reasons

John Aldridge scores against Latvia.

Denis Irwin
at Lansdowne
Road against
Lithuania.

already outlined; and against that background, we can't expect too many favours when we go to Belfast.

I truly wish it could be different, but I see little or no possibility of the two of us qualifying. On my reckoning then, Billy's lads will be playing just for their pride by the time we arrive at Windsor Park, but I don't expect it will be any easier for us because of that.

On the last occasion we played at the ground we had to settle for a scoreless draw, and my gut feeling is that they will again make it hard for us this time. My hope is that by that stage, we will have put enough points on the board to render the result of no significance. But only time will tell if I'm right.

26 · May · 1992

The older you get, they say, the quicker the time goes, and I can vouch for that today. It seems no time since we finished our European championship qualifying programme – in fact, the finals of that competition have yet to be played in Sweden.

Yet, here we are about to kick off another World Cup programme against Albania at Lansdowne Road, and immediately after that, we leave for a three-match American tour. It's been an eventful season and for all the disappointment of not getting to the European finals, we're aiming to finish it in style.

These last couple of months have been hectic ones for travel. Part of my brief is to check out the opposition before we ever get to meet them; and while I don't find much pleasure in travelling to places which I'd prefer to ignore, it is undeniably an essential part of the job.

Already I've seen Spain, Albania, Latvia and Lithuania play, and my impression is that Lithuania, whom we will not meet for another year, is the best of the smaller teams. They've already been in action in Ireland, drawing 2-2 in Belfast, and I'm sure that scoreline was a bit of an eye opener to people other than those in Northern Ireland.

Goals from Kevin Wilson and Noel Taggart had the home team comfortably in control in the opening half hour, and at that point the only thing at issue seemed to be the margin of their win. Then, inexplicably, they lost their way and the Lithuanians didn't need a second invitation.

The thing which struck me most about that game was the free kick which Fridrikas drilled into the back of the Irish net. It was at least thirty-five yards out; so far in fact, that it was decided to put just two players into the 'wall'. And that proved to be a mistake.

A couple of months earlier, I had gone to watch Lithuania play Austria in a friendly game. They lost 4-0 to the Austrians, but that was a distorted scoreline. In my book, it could have gone 5-4 either way. But one of the things imprinted on my mind from that game, is the memory of this Lithuanian guy stepping up and hitting a free kick with enormous power. It struck something before bouncing on to the crossbar and going over the top; but it was impressive enough to be remembered.

Billy Bingham chose not to go to that game. Had he done so he would never have allowed his players to build such a pathetic 'wall' and present Fridrikas with the chance to score. For me, it proved yet again the value of doing your homework thoroughly.

My journeys in the earlier months of the year also took me to Seville, where I saw Spain beat Albania 3-0. In the end it was clear-cut enough, but the Albanians had a couple of chances early on which, if taken, might have produced a vastly different result.

Armed with that information, I certainly wasn't taking anything for granted when the Albanians touched down in Dublin; but I must say that I wasn't quite prepared for a situation in which their list of deprivations stretched to the point where they arrived without footballs.

I think everybody is aware of the problems they are having in Albania. To this extent the FAI had no hesitation in lending them money to help them through their cash flow problems. But when a team travels without footballs, then you're getting close to rock bottom.

They were also short of playing gear, and that produced an interesting little cameo in the Under-21 game, immediately before the big match. Tony O'Sullivan, who works for Adidas in Ireland, duly provided them with a kit once their plight became known, and the visitors, it seemed, were suitably grateful.

Imagine O'Sullivan's surprise then when the Albanians ran out for the Under-21 game with a different set of tops to those he had given them. Everybody is entitled to his or her pound of flesh, and for the next five minutes or so, we were treated to the spectacle of Tony dashing around the pitch and in some cases physically ensuring that the Albanians wore exactly what he told them to wear.

In fact, we learned later that the Albanian players were pretty good at acquiring new gear, and far from being a one-off, their Dublin

experience was repeated several times subsequently.

The other big talking point in the run up to the game was the implementation for the first time at a game in Dublin of FIFA's new rule, banning standing spectators at competitive internationals. The thinking behind the new legislation is to force clubs and national associations to modernise stadiums, and by installing more seating, reduce the risk of violence at games.

Everybody is in favour of ridding football of thuggery, but I'm not so sure if the idea to ban standing spectators at games is a good one. The core support for football came from such people in the old days, and I believe there should be facilities for fans who simply cannot afford expensive seats.

My teamsheet for the game held few surprises. Mick McCarthy had his usual quota of injury problems coming up to the game, and in the circumstances I decided to go with a partnership of Paul McGrath and David O'Leary in central defence.

Packie Bonner was still in goal and that, I knew, would find favour with all those people who had come to regard Packie as something of a folk hero after his role in Italia '90 and, in particular, his save in the penalty shoot-out against Romania in Genoa.

The big man had known his problems at club level during the season just ending, but at international level his record is formidable. After twelve years or more in the international grade, he was still as keen as mustard for the challenge, and that pleased me.

By now, Roy Keane is beginning to make an impact with Ireland, and at right-back there was the familiar name of Denis Irwin. Ironically, there was a time when my old mate at Leeds United, Billy Bremner, didn't think much of Irwin. That was during Billy's term as manager at Elland Road. At the end of the 88/89 season, he allowed him to leave on a free transfer.

That kind of thing can break a young player; but in Denis's case, it merely provided him with one more reason to succeed in English football. He was lucky, perhaps, inasmuch as Joe Royle, the manager of Oldham Athletic, came in for him almost immediately, and what a shrewd signing that turned out to be.

Whereas he had seldom got the chance of putting a lot of games back to back with Leeds, Oldham provided him with first-team status almost immediately, and how Denis reacted to that situation. He simply got better and better under Joe Royle's tutorship, and by the time he left for United, there were few better full-backs in England.

One way or another then, I was delighted to have both Denis Irwin and Roy Keane in my team. At left-back I had no hesitation whatever in going again with a player I had long since come to admire, Steve Staunton.

I suspected that my defence was never going to be overworked on the day, for unless I was patently wrong, the Albanians had travelled for a point and would seek to close up the game at every opportunity. As it turned out, I was spot on with my assessment.

Many of the Albanian players are involved with clubs in western Europe and, not surprisingly, they have picked up all the tricks of the trade. They are particularly effective in operating the offside trap and time out of number John Aldridge and Niall Quinn were caught in it.

A couple of odd refereeing decisions didn't help us, and when we were allowed to get on with the game and run at them, we discovered that the Albanian goalkeeper was having a 'blinder'. No matter how the ball came at him, he was invariably in a position to keep it out.

In those circumstances it turned out to be a difficult enough day for us, and I realised yet again that in modern international football there is no such thing as an easy touch. The irritating thing was that if we struck early, I felt we could have ended up winning by three or four, and in a sense that merely heightened the tension in the wait for that vital opening goal.

We were well into the second half without any sign of the Albanians cracking, when I decided that we needed to change the direction of the game. In a situation in which we could have done with more leadership, I brought in Mick McCarthy, and within eight minutes of his arrival as a replacement for Kevin Sheedy, we made the breakthrough on the hour.

Like the others, Roy Keane had been having his problems in breaking down their defence; but then suddenly it happened. He chipped a ball from the edge of the box, and Aldo, doing everything right, timed the run so well that his header was in the net before the 'keeper realised it.

Once the Albanians had been broken, the rest was easy enough, and eight minutes later we were in for a second. McGrath jumped between two defenders to score with a powerful header from all of sixteen yards.

A 2-0 scoreline was not a true reflection of what had been a one-sided game, but it was a lot better than what looked likely at one stage. Albania, for all their deficiencies, had fought the good fight and we were convinced that there would be no favours available to us on the road to the United States in 1994.

 Roy Keane takes on the Lithuanian defence at Lansdowne Road.

 Tony Cascarino tries to get the ball under control in the home match against Lithuania.

9 · June · 1992

The idea of an end of season tour of the United States was probably first mentioned early in 1992. Sadly, we had failed to make the cut for the finals of the European championship, and in that situation we had no summer commitments.

The choice was to give the lads an extra fortnight's holiday, or alternatively, to take them on tour. I decided to leave the decision to the players and at a remove of four or five months they opted for the tour.

At that point they were up to their necks in cup and championship football in Britain, and the prospect of a nice leisurely tour seemed very attractive. It was a judgment which they, like me, would later question very seriously.

In fairness, I was probably guilty of misleading them. My information was that it was a low-key tournament, designed specifically to help the United States with their team-building plans for the World Cup finals. We had been to America the previous year for a match with the Yanks and enjoyed the experience so much that the lads couldn't wait to get back.

As it transpired, we were misled. Far from being low key, the tournament featuring Italy, Portugal, ourselves and the US was televised in several countries, including Ireland. That upped the pressure considerably, and by the time it was over I was sorry that I hadn't taken the team to some place like Majorca.

We left the day after the Albanian game and that was to prove of some significance. We had won the game we wanted to win and as such, the matches which followed were of even less consequence – or so it seemed!

My instructions to the players were clear.

They were just coming to the end of a long, difficult season and I wasn't going to impose on them further. All I asked was that they give me the day before each of the three games and, of course, the match day. The rest of the time was their own.

On one point however I was emphatic. The players would have to be in their rooms by 10.30 the night before a game and, obviously, booze was off limits that evening. The lads accepted that, but almost immediately we ran into trouble. A lot of drink was apparently consumed on the flight to Washington, but since I was at the front of the Jumbo, I wasn't aware of what was happening further down the plane.

Then, when we got to Washington we were whisked off to a fund-raising dinner and that certainly didn't help. One way or another it was a long, long day, and with the first tour game coming up in just forty-eight hours, it was not the ideal preparation to start a tour.

Even now, I'm not quite certain if it was the booze, the time differential adjustment, or the fact that there just weren't enough hours to recover; but whatever the reason, we didn't perform that night in the Robert Kennedy Stadium.

I had taken twenty players with me; but for two of them, Kevin Sheedy and Roy Keane, the tour was over almost before it started. Sheedy didn't play at all because of a knee problem; and when Keane retired with a dodgy ankle in the second half of the American game, I knew that he was gone for the other two matches.

The plan was to give everybody in the squad a game, and for the first match I decided to turn things round a little and go with five midfield

 John Sheridan in action against the Spaniards.

Terry Phelan controls the ball despite the challenge from Spain's Voro at Lansdowne Road.

 Spain's Nadal beats Niall Quinn to the ball during our 3-1 defeat at home to Spain.

runners and just one specialist striker, Niall Quinn. Events would prove that it wasn't the wisest team selection I ever made, but we still played some good football on a tight, unhelpful pitch.

There was a lot of good running from midfield, but with the rain pelting down, there was just no way that we could get the ball to stop. And instead of winning the game as our record suggested, we ended up, painfully, on the wrong end of a 3-1 scoreline.

It started out promisingly enough for us with Mick McCarthy heading the opening goal early in the second half, but then things began to go radically wrong. Hugo Perez equalised just three minutes later, and before we quite realised it, Marcello Balboa had the Americans in front.

Then, perhaps for the first time in the game, we began to put it together and created at least two good chances. Unfortunately, both of them got away and before the end John Harkes the Sheffield Wednesday player, rubbed salt into an open wound with a third goal for the home team.

It was a bad start to our programme, not so much for the fact that we lost the game, but rather that we failed to convert some good opportunities. A lot of people were impressed by the Americans, but I felt that with the right attitude and a full team, we'd take care of them if we met again.

The next game against Italy, some five days later, took us to Foxboro just outside Boston. Our first match had attracted a crowd of 36,000 and in spite of our defeat there was another bumper attendance for the Italian fixture.

Before the game I was told that Ireland, incredibly, had never beaten Italy, and deep down I suspected that history was about to repeat itself in Foxboro. It wasn't that I considered our team to be inferior to theirs – more a question of attitudes and the fact that we had just lost a game that we should have won.

It was a warm sunny day in Foxboro when the teams came out and there seemed to be just as many Italian supporters as Irish inside the stadium. It made for an unusual setting for a friendly game, but there was never any question of anybody passing out because of tension or too much excitement.

Once again, Italy won with their two goals coming from a penalty and a free kick. Apart from that, they didn't cause us any real problems, but then again we failed to create anything in their penalty area.

It was useful to play against the Italians and discover that we could cope with their style, but I reckon the thing that people will remember most about the game was the incident in the second half which led to the sending off, for the first time ever, of Packie Bonner.

Giuseppe Signori had put them in front in the seventeenth minute after a free kick, and that score was still the only one in the game when Signori, yards offside, was allowed to run in on Bonner. But instead of knocking the ball past him, he checked and tried to take it across him. In fact, that is not quite right either. Once Packie confronted him, he 'dived' – and the referee 'bought' it.

Acting on the rule book, the referee awarded a penalty and then, almost in the same action, he reached into his back pocket for a red card and Packie was off. Bonner was absolutely furious about that decision and I can't say I blame him.

His point was that if an opponent runs at a goalkeeper there is no way, short of stepping to one side, that the 'keeper can avoid making contact with that player. When that happens, he finds himself doubly disciplined – firstly the concession of a penalty and then a red card. How can a man of thirteen or fourteen stone vanish into thin air? Referees will invariably penalise the 'keeper in that situation.

I agree with Packie in what he says, but my big complaint on this occasion was that Signori should 'dive' in a friendly game. It's a despicable tactic at any time, but whatever about the merits of 'conning' people in a World Cup or European championship match, it is stretching things a bit far when players do it in a match which counts for little or nothing.

To make things worse, Signori was, as I said, clearly in an offside position when the ball was played to him. But then again, it wasn't all that surprising that he got away with it. We found out afterwards that the referee and both his linesmen were of Italian extraction.

Two games and two defeats didn't add up to much of a party that night. Early next morning, a Friday, Andy Townsend came to see me. We were due to meet Portugal in Foxboro on the Sunday and Andy's message for me couldn't have been simpler and, from my point of view, more reassuring.

He said that our team had deservedly acquired a reputation as one of the hardest to beat in international football and that we were now damaging that reputation by our approach to the whole American tour. He said that he had talked the problem through with the rest of the players and that they would prepare properly for the Portuguese match.

I said, 'Fine, but that means training starts right now.' To be fair, they were as good as their word, and once I had seen them train and sensed the different attitude, I knew that it was going to be a whole new ball game on Sunday.

I brought in Alan McLoughlin in midfield in place of Townsend, who looked absolutely jaded against the Italians. Chris Morris was at right-back in place of Denis Irwin and with an eye to the future, I played Terry Phelan on the left side of midfield.

The Portuguese hadn't exactly set the place alight with the quality of their performances in the US, but they had a lot of big-name players in their squad. Like us, they may not have given their tour a lot of attention, but whatever the reason, they were never better than second best in our match.

Steve Staunton put us ahead directly from a corner kick shortly before half-time, and we should have had a few more before Tommy Coyne went low to knock in a cross from Eddie McGoldrick two minutes from the end.

Thus ended a tour which in retrospect we should never have undertaken. That is not to say that it didn't have its merits. With so many competitive fixtures looming up, it gave us the opportunity to try out a few things here and there.

Friendly games are the means by which people like me blood new players, so that they don't feel totally out of place when they're selected for competitive matches. They provide managers with the opportunity to experiment, and to that extent they should not be taken into account when the records of managers are being assessed.

Yet overall, I think it was a mistake to have gone to the United States for what proved to be no more than a fistful of dollars. It was an unnecessary imposition on players at a time when they could have done with a holiday.

This is not to be unappreciative of the support and good-will which the Irish population in the States gave us. But as long as I'm manager of the team, we shall not be repeating that three-match programme.

9 · September · 1992

When the draw for the World Cup preliminaries was made last December, there was precious little I knew about Latvia, and even less about its football team. But even at that stage, I was prepared to gamble that they would not be among the strongest sides in the group.

Normally, it is possible to get a line on the strength of a team, even if you've never seen them play. But in this instance that simply wasn't possible. The break-up of the old Soviet Union shifted the balance of power in eastern European football and left at least three 'springers' in the draw for the World Cup.

It was our luck to be grouped with two of them, but it didn't take me long to figure that Lithuania was likely to be more of a handful for us than the Latvians, who, I discovered, did not have a great footballing tradition.

In my book, it was important to get points in the bank early, and having seen off the Albanians in our first qualifying game in May, I was looking for another home win to boost our spirits, before venturing abroad for those two difficult games in Denmark and Spain.

That said, it was difficult to ignore the fact that just a fortnight earlier they had gone and put a big hole in Denmark's challenge by taking a point off them in Riga. From a distance of some 1,500 miles or more, that result truly shocked me.

I had watched Denmark win the European championship in Sweden in the summer, and if somebody had said to me then that they would drop a point against Latvia, I would simply not have believed him. But in football there is no such thing as a soft touch these days, and the Latvians made the point perfectly in that match in Riga.

From our point of view it made the job a little more difficult, for having put a spanner in the Danish works, they would now be that much more confident of saving a point in Dublin. Fortunately, the word on the bush telegraph was that a couple of their key players would struggle to be available for the trip to Ireland.

Even before I came over to Dublin, I knew that Ray Houghton was out of the game because of an injury. Even though he had struggled in some of our earlier games, Houghton's experience and his ability to make those sharp, incisive runs into the penalty area was still a key part of our game plan. Whatever about this game I urgently needed him for the fixtures coming up over the next couple of months.

If the resumption of our international programme brought disappointment to Razor, it had precisely the opposite effect for Ronnie Whelan, a man who had soldiered with him for so long in the days when they were team-mates at Liverpool.

As mentioned earlier, Whelan's on-going injury troubles had been a source of genuine regret to me. Back in my early years in charge of the Ireland team, he had been one of my most trusted players, a lad who could always be depended upon to give you one hundred per cent, home or away.

But starting with that fateful day when he broke a bone in his foot just a couple of months before the kick-off in Italia '90, his career had been knocked for six by a whole range of injuries which might have broken the spirit of a lesser man.

Ronnie is nothing if not a great competitor, and as he fought to save his career, I made it clear that there would be a place in the squad for him if he got himself back to full fitness. Now, after a reasonably settled run in Liverpool's team, he was about to cash in on that pledge and I was delighted for him.

It was a big day too for Alan Kernaghan, a young man who first came to my attention after he had written to the FAI pointing out that although brought up in Northern Ireland, he was eligible to play for the Republic under the ancestry rule. Players don't often show that kind of initiative, and I was impressed.

I had seen Alan play several times for Middlesbrough, and I liked what I saw. He was strong and authoritative in the air, and if not the quickest player around, he was fast enough to do the kind of job I had in mind for him.

After being spoiled for choice in the two centre-back positions for so long, I am realistic enough to admit that difficult days lie ahead. Each and every one of the centre-backs in the squad is over 30. By the time the World Cup finals take place in America, Kevin Moran will be 37.

It's asking a lot of any man to perform at the highest level at that age, and for all his big heart, I reckon Kevin won't be up to it. Accordingly, I left him out of the original squad, only to be forced into calling him up when David O'Leary withdrew.

I thought long and hard about putting Terry Phelan into the team for the start. At a time when some critics were questioning the pace in our defence, he had speed to burn. Moreover, he had shown in America that he was beginning to find his feet in international football.

After weighing up the pluses and minuses, however, I decided to stick with what I had, and after the usual training session on the Tuesday, I named Stephen Staunton at left-back, with Kevin Sheedy stationed immediately in front of him.

As it transpired the decision to play Sheedy was spot on. On a dry, sandy surface we put a lot of good moves together in the opening half, without ever getting their goalkeeper, Yuri Ionchine, into any kind of serious trouble.

Credit for that went in part to their two centre-backs, Oleg Alexeenko and Roland Bulders; but even allowing for their stonewalling display, we should not have had to wait so long for our opening goal. But invariably the final pass was never precise enough to clear a path through the middle of their defence.

In that situation we had good reason to thank Sheedy. Denis Irwin provided the cross in the 32nd minute, and as the defenders converged on John Aldridge, Kevin was given just enough space to hammer the ball home from close range. It was his ninth goal for Ireland, and if it scarcely compared in importance with the one he hit against England in the World Cup game in Cagliari three years earlier, it was still one to savour.

That fine strike sapped much of the tension from the game from our point of view, and as the players took more time on the ball, we dominated the Latvians to an even greater extent after half-time. Appropriately, it was Sheedy who set up the chance for our second goal, flighting a corner kick so accurately that Aldridge, on the burst, was able to pick his spot with the header.

That was vintage Aldo – and there was more to come. Tommy Coyne, who had come in for Niall Quinn on the hour, was going through

John Aldridge celebrates Paul McGrath's goal in the opening World Cup qualifying match against Albania at Lansdowne Road.

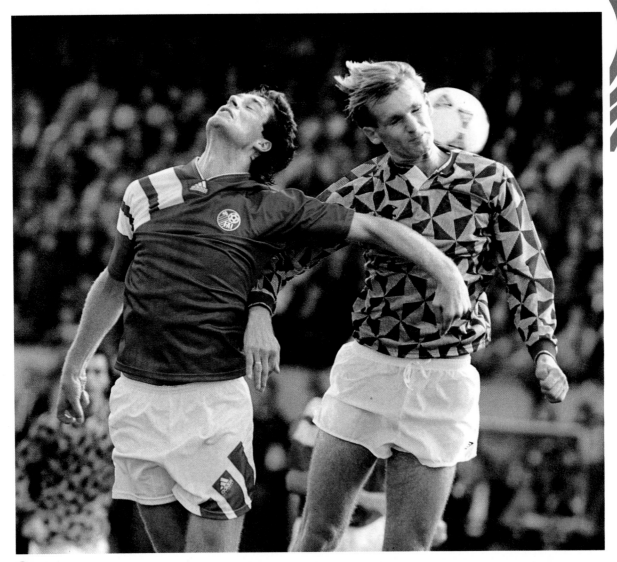

Niall Quinn and Bouldars jump together in the home match against Latvia.

when Bulders took him from behind and John, with that characteristic swagger, stitched the penalty kick into the corner of the net.

Roy Keane should have had another soon afterwards, but with four minutes left, the Latvian defence buckled again and Ionchine was stooping into his net to retrieve the ball for a fourth occasion. Again it was Irwin who hit the cross with such pace and accuracy, that Aldridge was able to climb above Einars Gnedoi and head the best goal of the day.

That completed John's hat-trick – the second of his international career – and just as he had done against Turkey two years earlier, he reaped the reward for quick thinking. There are those who believe that he has lost half a yard in pace over the last couple of years, but on this occasion at least, he showed himself to be as sharp as ever in the six yard area.

Given the way the game has developed at international level, a 4-0 scoreline represents a whopping win, but in view of all the scoring chances we made, I was disappointed we didn't score more. We could have done our goals difference column a lot of good in this game, and

the way things are developing we may live to regret those misses.

In my opinion, Alan Kernaghan had an excellent Ireland debut. Admittedly there wasn't too much pressure put on him, but I liked the way he adapted to the pace of the game. The only downside about his performance was the fact that he picked up a yellow card.

Paul McGrath, as ever, played with a lot of authority and taken in conjunction with Kernaghan's contribution, that was an encouraging augury for next month's assignment in Copenhagen, where we will surely need all our resources under pressure to stay afloat.

Midfield as ever is going to be crucial against the Danes, and I think we saw enough in the second half of the Latvian game to suggest that Roy Keane and Andy Townsend are capable of enabling us to trade on level terms in that area.

For the moment, however, I am resolved to enjoy the fruits of a good day's work. They won't all be as easy as this, but that shouldn't interfere with the celebrations. After all, that intimidating journey to Copenhagen will be upon us soon enough.

14 · October · 1992

In all my time in football, I have not experienced a more electrifying atmosphere in a ground than that in Copenhagen's new National Stadium on the night we put our World Cup dreams on the line against Denmark.

Maybe it was the rain, slanting down like stair rods, which accentuated the noise, but the sound inside that stadium as we walked down along the touchline to await the kick-off was something else.

Out there, among the crowd, were probably as many as 8,000 Irish supporters, a vast number when you consider the expense and trouble of travelling between Ireland and Denmark at that time of the year.

They know the importance of the prize at stake. Ever since the draw was made, it's been clear that the away games against Denmark and Spain would hold the key to the success of our qualifying programme.

If we did well in either or both of these fixtures, we would have a reasonable chance of making it through to the finals. If we lost both, it would heighten the pressure for the return matches in Dublin, and place a big question mark against our prospects of finishing in the top two.

What I didn't know at that point, of course, was that Denmark would be the champions of Europe by the time we met them. In fact, they hadn't even qualified to take part in the European finals at the time the World Cup draw was being made.

What happened next was truly one of the most unlikely stories in the entire history of international football. Because of the civil war then being waged in their country, Yugoslavia were unable to travel to the finals and were replaced by the second placed team in the group, Denmark.

That didn't happen until pretty close to the finals in Sweden, and in theory, it ought to have left Richard Moeller Nielsen, their manager, with little or no time in which to prepare a team. In fact, it worked in precisely the opposite direction. Whereas those teams which had qualified eight months earlier were caught up in all the tension in the countdown to the big occasion, the Danes went to Sweden completely relaxed.

They were there, ostensibly, to make up the numbers. If they didn't win a game, so what! They weren't supposed to be there in the first place. Conversely, every point gained was a bonus, and in that situation they went from strength to strength.

I was in Sweden working as a match analyst for ITV and, like everybody else, I marvelled at the way the Danes grew in confidence to the point where they were able to look Germany in the eye in that memorable 2-0 win in the final.

Mind you, I had long been an admirer of the way they played the game. When they had the ball, it was pretty difficult to take it from them. Anything you got against Denmark you earned.

Besides, they had some marvellous individuals scattered through their team, people who on any given day could lift those around them. Brian Laudrup of Fiorentina was one such player.

For years his brother Michael had been recognised as one of the finest talents in European football. Now the younger member of the family was showing the way for Denmark, a pacey, imaginative player who could change the course of a game in just a couple of seconds.

Kim Vilfort and the great Lars Olsen were others who commanded the respect of opponents anywhere they went, and behind them, of course, was Peter Schmeichel, an imposing goalkeeper, who had looked virtually unbeatable in the European finals in the summer.

Ranged against this kind of talent, we would have to play out of our skins to get a good result. And, of course, it didn't help that we had to take them on without Paul McGrath. It meant that Kevin Moran was back in central defence and alongside him I played Alan Kernaghan.

Apart from getting that yellow card against Latvia, Kernaghan had done exceptionally well in his first international game. Admittedly the opposition wasn't the greatest, but I was taken by the way he adapted to the new challenge. The fact that McGrath was around to take care of him was invaluable and now, with Paul marked absent, I wondered how Alan would fare in this, one of the most demanding of all international assignments.

Moran is a man whom I admire intensely. There are, conceivably, better players on the international scene, but none braver, none that

Eddie
McGoldrick
and John
Aldridge
(below) in
action in the
first major
test of the
qualifying
campaign,
the away
game to
Denmark.

Lopez foils John Aldridge in the drawn game in Seville.

Andy Townsend coming out against Spain in Seville.

Ray Houghton and Manuel Lopez contest the ball in Seville.

you would rather have in there battling for you when the going got tough, as it inevitably did on occasions like these.

When I took over the Ireland job, I was lucky to have lads like Kevin Moran around me. They gave me the stability I needed when I was building the squad. And in the course of the 1988 European championship in Germany, and again in Italy two years later, they showed that they could compete at the highest level.

But time marches on and I fear that Kevin has now reached a stage in his career where he's going to find it increasingly difficult to get to the pace of the game. I just hoped that those fears would not be substantiated in Denmark.

Apart from the absence of Paul McGrath, I had another pressing problem. Steve Staunton was out injured, and with Kevin Sheedy also in trouble, I had to reorganise the left flank of the team. It meant that Terry Phelan started a competitive international game for the first time with Eddie McGoldrick playing out of position on the left side of midfield.

Staunton, in particular, is a big loss, for he gave us something extra going forward. He is generally a sweet striker of the ball, and while he still has a lot of self-doubt when asked to go past opponents, I believe that he has the ability to develop still further.

Against that, I liked what I saw of Phelan in the game against the United States in Washington in June, and McGoldrick has filled so many roles for Crystal Palace that I reckon one more is not going to hurt him.

Noise apart, the most notable feature of the National Stadium on the match night was the scarcity of grass on the pitch. In every other respect the arena is impressive, but for some strange reason they've had problems in getting grass to grow there.

Before the game, I stressed the importance of settling into the game early and not allowing the Danes to develop any fluency. If they were allowed to run the game from the kick-off, there was a real threat of our midfield being swamped and that could lead to only one result.

In the event, I think it was the Danes who were in danger of being overrun in the first half. Right from the kick-off, Andy Townsend and Roy Keane dug in to take control in midfield, and with Ray Houghton and Eddie McGoldrick getting to the end line on a couple of occasions, we began to turn the screw on their defence.

I bet Moeller Nielsen wasn't prepared for that situation – and neither was Smeichel after Paul McGrath, challenging fairly for the ball, had left him in an untidy bundle on the grass.

We possibly deserved a goal from that early barrage, but unfortunately from our point of view there was nothing doing. Townsend had a 'squeak' midway through the first half when he headed narrowly wide, and after that McGoldrick got in behind the defence only to shoot over the top.

We needed a goal from either or both of those incidents and when it failed to materialise the Danes began to grow in confidence. For the first time in the game, Kim Vilforth and John Jensen began to look menacing in midfield, and as they came more into the game, Laudrup was given the chance to run at our defence.

Apart, however, from a well-struck shot which Packie saved and another good run which ended with Kevin Moran making a timely interception, we kept our net intact without too much stress, and by the time the Polish referee blew the whistle, I felt they had settled for a point.

My initial reaction, naturally, was one of

delight. There were occasions in the first half when we played well enough to hold out hope of winning the match; but overall, a draw was perhaps the fairest result.

For all the Danes' problems since returning from Sweden, it is still an achievement to hold them scoreless at home, and later in the evening we enjoyed another boost when word came through from Belfast that Northern Ireland had drawn with Spain.

Analysing our performance on the journey back to Dublin, I tended to dwell longest on the contribution of Kevin Moran. Before the game I had my reservations about Kevin's ability to dominate as in the old days, and I'm delighted to say that I was wrong.

The man played as if he'd never been away, and in a game in which our backs were to the wall in the last half-hour, he was simply superb. Whatever about his first-eleven claims, it is clear that he must come back into the squad as a regular.

I was taken, too, by the way Terry Phelan handled the occasion. His game is all about pace and positional sense, and the Danes' tactics suited him perfectly. Opponents who attack by going over the top will give him the occasional problem, but there is no better defender against those one-twos which the Europeans play so well.

There was one occasion, it seemed to me, where he even outpaced Laudrup. And there are very few defenders in the game who can make that sort of claim. Eddie McGoldrick also did well in trying circumstances, but once again the night was spoiled for us by a second yellow card for Alan Kernaghan.

Admittedly that booking was the direct result of an earlier mistake by Niall Quinn, but the fact remains that it was Alan's name which went into the notebook. And coupled with his earlier indiscretion against Latvia, it means that he'll miss next month's meeting with Spain in Seville.

18 · November · 1992

The prospect of playing Spain in Seville appealed to me from day one. It didn't take a genius to deduce after the various groupings had been made, that our toughest games would be those in Spain and Denmark.

Although I wasn't to know then that the Danes would be rejoicing in the title of European champions by the time we played them, I respected them as a fine team with some gifted individual talent to lift their level of performance.

The Spaniards, too, were a formidable force and I was determined that I would meet them as early in the season as possible when my players were still fresh.

Although I didn't make too much of it at a pre-match press briefing, I had another reason for pulling out all the stops in Seville.

Four years earlier, I had gone there with a badly depleted team and suffered the disappointment of being beaten 2-0.

On the face of it, the scoreline wasn't too bad, but deep down it hurt. It's a funny business this football management, but you're always hoping for little miracles. You know in your heart of hearts that you haven't a prayer and yet you advance a dozen different reasons why you might, just might, win.

Going to Seville in November 1988, I knew I

Roy Keane in action in the home match against Northern Ireland.

was on a hiding to nothing. Half the team were unavailable through injury and I ended up playing Kevin Moran alongside Liam O'Brien in midfield. Now Kevin is one of the most committed and willing players I know, but a central midfielder? Never! And yet, somehow, I clung to the hope that the gamble would pay off.

It didn't. We got a bit of a run-around that night, and leaving the ground, I vowed that I would go back there with a full-strength team at some point in the future and show those Spaniards who was the boss.

In saying that, I wasn't losing sight of the fact that Seville is something of a football fortress. The fanatical support for the Spanish team there is worth almost a goal start.

The other thing I recall from that ill-fated visit of four years ago was the nerve of the Spanish Federation in depositing us in a hotel which was a long way out of the city centre. As I recall it, we seemed to spend hours in traffic jams when we needed to leave the hotel, and after a while that began to grate on people.

This time we insisted on staying downtown, just a couple of hundred yards from the Ramon Sanchez Stadium, where the match is to be played. This is the bigger of the two stadiums in Seville and it's odd to think that within weeks of playing in the European finals in Germany in 1988, the Spaniards in their wisdom saw fit to shunt us to the smaller one.

Now, apparently, our reputation has grown to the point where they reckon we merit the honour of playing in the Ramon Sanchez arena. The other consideration, of course, was FIFA's insistence that only seated spectators would be permitted at competitive international games.

The effect of that ruling on attendances at Lansdowne Road threatens to be profound, but the Spaniards, typically, sidestepped the regulations by painting the terraces on which spectators normally stood, and claiming that each division represented a seat. It broke the spirit, if not the wording of the new legislation, but they got away with it. I doubt if we'd have been so lucky if we had tried the same thing.

The selection of our team was pretty straightforward. Alan Kernaghan, booked for the second successive game in Copenhagen last month, had to sit this one out; but with Paul McGrath fit and primed for action again, it didn't weaken us unduly. Kevin Moran had done well against the Danes, and in a situation in which we might find ourselves under the cosh I had every confidence in him.

Also back in the side was Steve Staunton – and that, too, pleased me. Eddie McGoldrick hadn't done at all badly against the Danes and clearly he rated as one of our better prospects for the future. But this I felt was a job for experienced international players and I was delighted to have Steve with me.

As in Denmark, I resolved that we just wouldn't sit back and soak up punishment. We'd have a go at them when the opportunity presented itself. There was no question of us going out to pepper them from the kick-off – that would have been suicidal – but I reckoned we had now matured to the point where we were capable of going after teams and showing our teeth in games away from home.

According to the Spaniards, there were only 45,000 fans in the stadium, but from where I stood and listened, that figure was conservative. In among them were some 8,000 Irish supporters, and I think they got their money's worth.

As planned, we ran the Spaniards when we got the chance, and it should have brought us a goal after only 22 minutes. Roy Keane pushed the ball through; John Aldridge stepped over it and suddenly, there was Niall Quinn on his own, bearing down on goal.

These are the kinds of situations which strikers both love and hate. It's a marvellous feeling for them when the ball finishes in the net. But if it stays out, they wish that the ground would open up and swallow them. In this instance, Niall appeared to have committed the 'keeper Zubizarreta to the wrong direction, but at the last second he stuck out his foot and deflected the ball just wide of an upright.

Niall couldn't believe it and, to be honest, neither could I. We were entitled to expect to go one up in that instance and when it didn't happen for us, I turned to Maurice Setters and the unspoken message was that this might be one of those nights when our luck was out.

Yet, both Maurice and I were agreed that we were going about the job in the right way, and generally giving the Spaniards a taste of their own medicine. We were moving the ball around confidently, tying things up nicely at the back and, on balance, giving more than we got.

But two incidents were to deny us a victory. The first, in the 56th minute, involved the Atletico Madrid player, Lopez, who had been giving John Aldridge a bit of stick since the start of the game. Aldo, as is his custom, put his head down and got on with the job regardless. In a moment of superb skill, he looked to have got his revenge.

Swivelling on a pass from Roy Keane, he turned past Lopez before the Spaniard quite realised what was happening, and was gone. For a split second the stadium froze as Aldo made tracks on goal. As I saw it, he was already inside the penalty area when Lopez brought him down

from behind.

Instinctively, the referee reached into his back pocket for the red card to punish the professional foul. But in his determination to punish Lopez, he seemed to forget that the incident took place inside the area. In sending off the Spaniard he did us no favours, for I believe we should have had a penalty.

That dismissal should have given us an extra edge, but of course football doesn't work as logically as that. The Spaniards redeployed their players shrewdly, but we were still making the running when the second big turning point occurred.

Roy Keane knocked the ball in from the right; Niall Quinn touched it on, and for the third time in the game, it was a one-on-one situation as Zubizarreta looked up at Aldo bearing down on him. John, holding his nerve, took the ball around him and then measured the angle neatly to put the ball into the empty net.

The referee at first turned as if to run back to the centre. But glancing at one of his linesmen, he stopped and I knew immediately that the goal wasn't going to stand. The linesman had flagged Aldridge for offside. The referee, despite his earlier enthusiasm for the score, accepted the flag without demur, and for all our protests there was no way he was about to change his mind.

I was aggrieved and so was every Irish supporter in the stadium. I rushed back to the team hotel after the game to watch the video, and sure enough, there was a Spanish defender between the goalkeeper and Aldo when Quinn played the ball. To give the Spanish television commentators their due, they made no attempt to minimise the referee's error.

That was the second raw deal we had from the referee, and the effect was to be profound. We

Tony Cascarino in action against the Danes at Lansdowne Road.

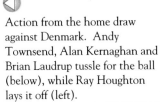

Action from the home draw against Denmark. Andy Townsend, Alan Kernaghan and Brian Laudrup tussle for the ball (below), while Ray Houghton lays it off (left).

played well enough on the night to be worth a win, but instead of the two points we deserved, we had to content ourselves with one.

Not only were we the better team, but I think everybody in the stadium knew that we also had the best player – Roy Keane. Young Roy was fantastic, running all night and doing things which others found next to impossible. Despite all the talk about the player in the British and Irish press for the last couple of years, the Spaniards, it seemed, were unprepared for him.

Whereas Roy is pushed for space any time he plays a club game in England, his Spanish marker was prepared to give him the freedom of the park, and he accepted it. Andy Townsend, too, had a great game in midfield and, no less than the others, he deserved better for his night's labours.

To be absolutely fair, the Spaniards themselves might have sneaked in for a winner. Just before the end, Jose Bakero came steaming in on the blindside and just missed making contact by a matter of inches. Had he done so the ball might well have ended up in the net, and the final injustice of the night would have been perpetrated.

To that extent, the scoreless draw wasn't wholly unacceptable. We were, without question, the better team and I figure Javier Clemente, the Spanish manager, knew it. Even now I suspect that they will be intimidated psychologically when they come to Dublin for the return game.

31 · March · 1993

In preparing for our game against Northern Ireland in Dublin, I found it difficult to banish the memories of the previous occasion we had met them at Lansdowne Road, back in 1979.

On that occasion, we swarmed all over them in the first half-hour without ever putting the ball in their net and, as I recall, it took a good goal by Ronnie Whelan to get us back on track.

This time, I resolved that we would get the job done as soon as possible, spare ourselves the tension that invariably sets in when you attack for a long time without scoring, and generally give the Dublin public the kind of entertainment they expect to see.

Because of an agreement worked out between the FAI and the IFA in Belfast, no tickets will be sold to northern fans for this game, with a corresponding arrangement for our last qualifying match at Windsor Park in eight months' time.

I feel sorry for the genuine fans on both sides of the border, who will be denied the chance of cheering on their team because of the excesses of the few. But in the circumstances I think it is a sound decision by the two associations. Northern Ireland don't attract as much away support as we do, and I would hope that by the time the Belfast game comes around, we will already have made certain of our place in the finals in America, and that the majority of our followers will not feel the need to travel for this one.

For Billy Bingham, it's very much a make or break game. Because of their indifferent start to their programme, they've never really been on an even keel in this competition, and Billy knows that if he loses this one, there'll be no way back for either him or his players.

Instead of taking in our friendly game against Wales at Tolka Park the previous month, I decided to go to Tirana to watch Northern Ireland in action against Albania. This was the first time in seven years in the job that I had missed an Ireland senior game and I thought the circumstances warranted it.

For one thing, the Welsh match was a friendly and Maurice Setters would fill me in on anything I needed to know. The bigger, more pressing reasons were to check out conditions in Tirana in view of our game there in three months' time and also to get an update on Northern Ireland's form.

Even in the wake of the break-up of the old Soviet Union and the death of communism in eastern Europe, Albania was still a no-go area for people from the West. If we were going to play an important game there, it was essential to do our homework and experience at first hand the special difficulties of life in that unfortunate country.

Given the timescale, it was also imperative that we got a line on Northern Ireland's team. No less than the journalists who travelled with me on the trip, I thought they did extremely well to win 2-1.

The Albanians, I was told, didn't have all their best players in their team, but for my money they were sharp enough. Given that backdrop, I thought that Billy's lads did well to get out with two points.

As ever, Alan McDonald had a great game at centre-back, and I knew yet again that he would give us problems in Dublin. He's not the greatest in the world when made to turn, but attacking the ball he's immense, and most important of all, he lifts those around him.

Lads like Jim Magilton and Philip Gray, a newcomer to me, did well, but McDonald apart, the player who impressed me most was Tommy Wright in goal. He's developed into a fine international goalkeeper and he proved it that day with a string of precious saves.

When you've people like Wright and McDonald in the opposing defence, you know for sure that you're going to have to work pretty hard for anything you get. And yet I was agreeably surprised by the manner in which things went for us.

As in the match in Dublin four years earlier, we took the game to them from the kick-off. The difference on this occasion was that whereas the ball stayed out of their net through a mixture of good defence and bad finishing in the first game, we now got the big breakthrough at a relatively early stage.

Andy Townsend, looping around Niall Quinn, caught the volley a little clumsily, but from where I sat, it was always going to finish in the net. The goalkeeper, committed to the near post, could only stand and watch as the ball flew past him into the far corner.

That goal meant that unless we did something stupid at the opposite end of the pitch, we were going to leave with two points, and with that cushion we were able to express ourselves a lot more eloquently.

Conversely, it pulled the rug from under the Northern team, who were trading on the belief that the longer it took us to score the more frustrated we would become. That conviction had now gone out the window and with it many of their hopes of saving the game.

Goal number two gave me particular pleasure, for it resulted from something we had worked on in training. Niall Quinn is essentially a far-post

▷ Peter Schmeichel
looks ruefully at
the ball which has
beaten him for
Ireland's equaliser
(below), while our
lads congratulate
the scorer, Niall
Quinn (right).

Albania was a strange experience both for the fans (below) and for me.

player. But he is encouraged at every opportunity to come across his marker and get the vital touch with either his boot or his head at the near upright.

On this occasion, the ball was played in from the right, and the big man, timing the run superbly, cut across the defender to tuck the ball into the corner of the net with as neat a touch as you will ever see. From our point of view it was sheer poetry but, of course, it doesn't always go as smoothly or as effectively as that.

Shortly afterwards we went three in front – courtesy of Stephen Staunton's left boot. Apart from being a fine midfielder, Stan has the ability to take in-swinging corner kicks as well as anybody I've seen. That is why we dispatch him so often from the old left-half position to the opposite corner flag to try his luck with the placed ball.

Oddly enough, he didn't catch it particularly well and that was just as well, for had he done so the ball might well have ended up missing the far upright. But he cut this one slightly and, aided by the wind, it avoided a whole cluster of players and crept in at the near post.

At that point, I hoped and Billy Bingham feared, that we might run riot. After all, we're three in front, our confidence is flowing and, with a capacity crowd roaring us home, I figure that we can do our goals difference a lot of good in this game.

Curiously, we never get it right in the second half. Perhaps our players felt deep down that they had done enough for the day; or was it the arrival of Jimmy Quinn, or the fact that they were now

playing with the wind which made Northern Ireland more effective?

Whatever the reason, they looked a much better team after half-time and, without ever threatening to put one past Packie, they succeeded in denying us the kind of win which I considered a real possibility after just half an hour.

Yet, I couldn't be displeased. After extracting those two crucial points from the games in Denmark and Spain, we had now started back with a home win, and at this point our World Cup challenge is precisely on schedule.

In four weeks' time it will be the turn of Denmark to experience the special atmosphere of Lansdowne Road, and if we play as well then as we've just done, there will certainly be no complaints from me.

I shook Billy Bingham's hand as we left the pitch and, in a peculiar way, I thought he looked like a relieved man. Sure, the little miracle that he was looking for hadn't happened. But neither had the landslide which was a real possibility after Staunton had put away that third goal.

There was certainly nothing in Billy's face which suggested that he felt hard done by. We parted on good terms, and as we did so the home crowd was chanting, 'There's only one team in Ireland'. The fans up in Windsor Park might have something to say about that; but for the moment, at least, there can be little argument.

We beat them more comprehensively than even the scoreline indicated. In terms of morale, we couldn't be in better shape for that crunch meeting with the Danes!

28 · April · 1993

There were two big clouds on my horizon for the Denmark game in Dublin.

Kevin Moran, who had done so well in the games in Copenhagen and Seville, was struggling with a groin injury, and John Aldridge was having a bad time after tearing muscles in his stomach.

Sadly Kevin didn't make it, but I decided to gamble with Aldo – and immediately sparked off a controversy in the press. John had played only 30 minutes of football in the preceding six weeks, and the speculation was that he wouldn't be ready to handle a game of this importance.

I have to say that I wasn't too happy either with the player's build-up to the game, but having weighed up the situation, I decided I'd go with Aldo and hope that his experience and competitive instincts would get him through the game without too much difficulty.

In taking that line, I was influenced by the certainty that we were going to have to work uncommonly hard for anything we got out of the game. Denmark are past masters when it comes to keeping possession. If they have the ball, it's pretty difficult to get it back from them.

There was a time, back in my early days in the Ireland job, when I spent long hours trying to explain – not very successfully, it seemed – just what I expected of John Aldridge when he pulled on a green shirt. At the time, he was knocking in goals regularly for Liverpool, and supporters of the Irish team were mystified why he couldn't do the same for them.

The point they missed, of course, was that the two roles were vastly different. At Anfield, Liverpool could afford to leave John stationed in or around the penalty area, and depend on his sharp reflexes to do the rest.

With Ireland, Aldo soon discovered that he was required to do something different. Sure, we needed him to put the ball in the net. But apart from this, he was expected to work across the width of the park whenever the opposition had the ball.

Even though I as the taskmaster barked out the orders, I was the first to acknowledge the size of the job I was imposing on John. And to his eternal credit, he never flinched in accepting it.

Now, I needed him more than ever. If the Danes persisted in playing the ball back and forth between themselves, we had to have somebody who was prepared to go and retrieve it. And for all his shortage of match practice, Aldridge was the man to do that for us.

Before arriving in Dublin, Denmark had won just two of their qualifying games, scraping home 1-0 against Northern Ireland in Belfast before beating Spain with a similar scoreline in Copenhagen four weeks ago. Apart from the scoreless draw against us in October, they had dropped points in Latvia and Lithuania which must have astonished students of form. We expected better of teams which had just conquered Europe, and the Danes' failure to deliver simply defied football logic.

My own view is that having won the European title with a direct, old-fashioned brand of football, they started to believe their own publicity and got the notion that they were a good technical team – a view that wasn't shared by everybody who watched them floor the odds in Sweden.

Out there, they had pursued success through the simple expedient of bouncing the long

Kevin Moran rises high in Tirana.

Steve Staunton celebrates his goal in Tirana as Ireland win away.

John Aldridge celebrates the opening goal against Latvia in Riga.

 Paul McGrath accepts congratulations after scoring the second goal against Latvia away.

clearance off the opposing back four, and taking it from there. In all their games in the European finals, I cannot ever remember Peter Schmeichel rolling the ball to one of his defenders – and how right he was!

Immediately on their return home, however, the Danes began to view things differently. As European champions, they felt obliged to play the game like Germany, Holland or Italy, in other words, to move the ball through the middle.

It didn't work for them simply because they weren't used to the system but having suffered his criticism in silence, I felt that Richard Moeller Nielsen would abandon his delusions of grandeur and go back to basics for this assignment in Dublin. We based our pre-match preparations on that assumption and, as it turned out, we were spot on.

As in the first meeting with the Danes, we started better and put them under the kind of pressure which, on a day when your luck is running, might well have produced a goal. On at least two occasions, corner kicks by Denis Irwin and Stephen Staunton had Schmeichel in trouble, and then Ray Houghton beat the offside trap only to shoot past the far post.

At that point the crowd were in good voice for it seemed only a matter of time before a goal arrived. It came alright, in the twenty-seventh minute, but sadly not at the end of the ground we were attacking.

The Danes had scarcely mounted an attack of any significance when Lars Olsen 'hoofed' a ball in the general direction of our net. There wasn't a red shirt within ten yards of the action when Paul McGrath, unwittingly or otherwise, got his head to a ball which he should have left to Packie. The ball ran directly to Kim Vilforth, who looked up, saw Bonner off his line, and

volleyed the ball with fine precision into the roof of the net. What a goal for Denmark! What a bloody disaster for Ireland!

There is not a doubt in the world that Paul should have left that ball to the goalkeeper. But whether Packie called and Paul didn't hear him or whatever, we went a goal down to a team which, the Italians notwithstanding, was among the best in the world at protecting a lead.

They kept the ball so tightly among themselves that at times our players may have despaired of ever getting it back. To their credit, however, they never gave up the chase, and before half-time we might well have had a penalty when Marc Rieper blatantly fouled Niall Quinn.

But the referee stayed silent and we knew yet again that a hard slog lay ahead of us. The second half followed the same pattern, with the Danes showing no signs of losing their cool under pressure. Then, joyously, the sheer persistence of our attacks yielded an equaliser with only fifteen minutes to go.

Ray Houghton touched a short corner kick to Stephen Staunton on the right, and the inswinging cross was struck so sweetly that Niall Quinn barely had to rise to make the decisive contact at the near post and glance the ball with his head into the corner of the net.

It was the kind of situation at which we're good and which should bring us a lot more goals. Staunton is normally a good crosser of the ball and Quinn certainly has the finishing skills to make the best use of them.

After that, the game settled into a predictable pattern. The Danes were content to hold what they had, and while we pressed on in the hope of getting a winner, we seldom looked like doing it in the closing minutes.

My feelings immediately after the game were a mixture of relief and disappointment. In the sense that I went into the game fully expecting to win it, a 1-1 scoreline was a bit anti-climactic and cancelled out that excellent result in Copenhagen six months earlier.

Yet, given the situation which confronted us at the start of the last quarter, when Denmark was digging in with even more confidence than usual and we were beginning to look just a little bit ragged, I was happy enough with a point at the finish.

Above all else, we couldn't afford to lose at home, and if the manner in which we conceded the goal to Denmark was eating me up inside, it was consoling to know that over the two legs of the tie, we hadn't conceded anything to the European champions.

The scoreline did, however, have the effect of concentrating our minds for the difficult tests looming up in the months ahead. In the space of little more than a fortnight, we will play three away games in Albania, Latvia and Lithuania, and this result in Dublin has reduced our margin of error still further.

Ideally, I want a maximum of six points from those fixtures. At worst, we cannot afford to drop more than a point, and with that in mind I sent the players home to prepare themselves for one last supreme effort to round off the season.

Ominously, Roy Keane and Eddie McGoldrick joined those on yellow cards after being whistled up for relatively minor offences, and that is going to impose extra responsibilities on them to avoid a suspension during the remaining qualifying games.

All in all then, the pressure is beginning on every side as we head towards the half-way stage of our programme. It doesn't get any easier.

26 · May · 1993

The moment I walked into Tirana's International Hotel, I knew that my visit to the city with the Northern Ireland team some three months ago, and the flood of criticism which followed that game, had not been in vain.

In all my years in football, I had seldom seen a visiting team given such shabby treatment, literally and otherwise, as that meted out to Billy Bingham and his players. It earned the Albanian Federation a stinging rebuke from FIFA, and rightly so, for there must be minimum standards of hygiene and sanitation for any group of visitors to any country.

That said, the toilet in my hotel room still isn't working this time. But in almost every other respect things have improved. It is now possible to have a shower, the electricity works, a new carpet has been laid and, for a change, there are bodies behind the reception desk to deal with complaints.

Oh, one other thing. We have been given rooms on the second floor as opposed to the tenth floor, as was the case when Northern Ireland played here. A small point? Well, you try trudging up ten floors with luggage in the dark and with the carpet on the stairs all curled up, just for laughs.

In one other respect, we benefited from Northern Ireland's visit. They brought their food

 Action from the match in Riga. Paul McGrath heads the ball clear.

Ray Houghton gains control (left). The post-match interview with George Hamilton (below) is part of the normal match-day routine.

with them and a chef to prepare it, and it worked so well for Billy that I had no hesitation in recommending the idea for our visit.

The FAI, to its credit, came up trumps and in the space of our thirty-six hours in Tirana, they have served up something like 600 meals for the official party and supporters. In fact, the only complaint I have on this score was that they fed the players too well. For example, lunch for the players on a match day is usually nothing more than poached eggs on toast. When I discovered that they were preparing to set steak and chips before them, I nearly went through the roof.

To be fair, I felt much the same way before I ever got to Tirana. The Irish players were due to assemble in Dublin at noon on the Sunday, and they dutifully did – with one notable exception.

Paul McGrath rang up the hotel later in the day, and asked the telephonist who answered him to convey a message to me, to the effect that he had picked up a knee injury and would not be travelling with us to Albania.

I was hurt, not just because I was losing a good player, but because he didn't have the courtesy to tell me personally. I was in the hotel at the time he rang, and it would have been quite a simple matter to have put the call through to me. Perhaps he was afraid of what I might have told him.

I was totally unaware of his latest knee injury – after all, he hadn't played for the previous three weeks and if there was a problem, he had ample time to inform us of the situation. But in that period we didn't hear a word from him and now he had done a disappearing act, just three days before a World Cup game.

When he telephoned the hotel, he gave no indication as to where he was. We were aware that he had been involved in some promotional work in Cork the previous week. But when we enquired in that area about his whereabouts, we drew a blank.

Mick Byrne rang some of his friends. The friends contacted other acquaintances, and we even checked with his wife and his mother. But the answer was always the same – nobody had been in contact with him for the last two days!

At that point, I decided to cut our losses. It didn't matter a damn now whether Paul showed up or not; I wasn't going to play him. Alan Kernaghan and Kevin Moran would be my two centre-backs in Tirana and I would either stand or fall with them. Naming the rest of the team was a straightforward exercise. By this time, everybody knew my idea of our strongest eleven.

Unfortunately, the Albanians' teamsheet wasn't quite as straightforward. I had seen them play three times, made notes on all their players and felt as well prepared as I ever was by the time we set foot in Tirana. Imagine my surprise then on being handed a teamsheet that day before the match and recognising only three or four players on it.

For much of the previous eighteen months, we had been hearing how cash-strapped the Albanians were and how deprived the national team was. Yet, here they were at a stage of the competition when they were already out of contention, bringing back players from all over Europe to face us.

A journalist informed me that three of their best players were out because the Albanian Federation didn't have the money to insure them for the game; but as far as I was concerned, that was a load of rubbish. All the players whom I had noted as ones to watch were there. For me, this was the strongest team Albania had fielded from day one.

Fair enough! That is their prerogative. But in the interests of fair play, I believe that the Albanians should do precisely the same when they meet Spain and Denmark later in the year. If they don't, I intend to make certain that the FAI files a protest with FIFA.

The end product of the Albanians' decision to bring all their big guns to bear on us, is that I went into the game without a complete dossier on them. And that worried me, for in the modern game success is all about homework and careful planning.

I always respected the Albanians as sound technical players with a good first touch. And I sensed that if they got their nose in front, they could be desperately difficult to haul back. Prophetic or otherwise, my worst fears were realised within eight minutes of the kick-off.

Suleyman Demollari, on the turn, looked up to spot the chance and hit a tremendous thirty-yard pass for Sokel Kushta to chase. The Albanian, with first run on Alan Kernaghan, did not need a second invitation, and with Packie Bonner unable to make up his mind, Kushta fired it into the roof of the net.

From the Albanians' point of view, it was a tremendous score! From ours, it was something of a disaster – and I didn't hesitate to let the players know. People in football are no fools and by now everybody is aware of the way to play us. We tend to push up square from the back and if they want to get us into trouble, the way to do it is to hit the long ball over the top for people to chase.

Our answer to that is to close down the player about to make the pass and to put him under so much pressure that he doesn't have time to look up and pick out the player about to make the run. That didn't happen in Tirana and it gave Demollari the chance to do the damage.

A lot of people were ecstatic about Demollari that day. In a sense, it was a throw-back to the days of the old playmaker when players like John Giles sprayed passes all over the park and defenders suffered.

In the modern game the playmaker is redundant. And he's redundant because players no longer get the time and the space to do their thing. But in Tirana we rewound the clock and gave Demollari everything he needed to look a class operator.

Instead of putting balls in behind their defenders, we were playing them to their feet, and before sweat had broken it had cost us a goal. Some blamed Kernaghan for a shortage of pace, but while Alan is not the quickest player around I didn't see it that way.

Caught in that situation, any centre-back would get run – I've seen Des Walker in the same situation – but don't forget, Kushta didn't have to touch the ball until he was inside the area. I thought Packie could have done better, for had he come early there is no doubt that he would have got to the ball ahead of the Albanian.

From that point to half-time I fumed. We were not playing our normal game of pressuring the opposition, and my fear was that we would give away a second goal. In fact we nearly did, for it required a good tackle by Terry Phelan to prevent Kushta getting in again.

In conditions which didn't favour the running game – temperatures were into the high seventies – Roy Keane and Andy Townsend spared nothing or nobody. But I can tell you, it was a huge relief when Steve Staunton put us level directly from a free kick, shortly after Kushta's strike.

We are fortunate in having two brilliant dead ball kickers in Steve and Denis Irwin, and

Ray Houghton and Steve Staunton celebrate Staunton's goal against Lithuania away.

Sending Ronnie Whelan on as a substitute (below) and arguing with the officials (left) in Vilnius.

depending on the location of the free kick, they are equally lethal. On this occasion Denis was going to try to chip one over the top from twenty-five yards until Steve spotted a gap in the Albanian wall.

He told me afterwards that he couldn't believe his eyes when he saw how badly the wall was created and, good professional that he is, he stepped up and drove the ball at speed through the opening and into the corner of the net.

That was a real bonus, but we didn't build on it. With a lot of early fire leaving the Albanians' game we were well on top approaching half-time, but unfortunately the final ball was never sufficiently precise to produce a second score.

Half-time in our dressing room was something else. I couldn't wait to close the door to tell them how annoyed I was and how they were putting the game at risk by ignoring the basics. It's a long time since I had a go at them like this, but I reckon they deserved it.

This was a game in which we simply could not afford to slip. We needed two points urgently, but the way we were playing was not reassuring. I warned them that unless we pulled our socks up, there might be bitter tears shed at the finish.

To their credit they did what they had to do, and while the nation at large may have sat and fretted, I was always reasonably confident that we'd get the right result. Mind you, it was not until twelve minutes from the end that we snatched a winner; but overall, I thought we should have won more clearly.

In keeping with a game plan we had used so often in the past, I took John Aldridge off with 15 minutes to go and sent on Tony Cascarino to join Niall Quinn. Within 90 seconds of his introduction, Cass had scored and all Ireland was able to breathe freely again.

Again it was Staunton's accurate kicking which did the trick. This time he floated a corner kick to the far post and Cass met it firmly with his head to put it in the net. The Albanians protested furiously to the Italian referee – for what I do not know – but the score stood and we were in the lead.

Before the end, we had three good chances to score again, missed the lot and I wasn't impressed. Keane, on the burst, complained that the sun blinded him as he went for the simple header from Irwin's cross. Cascarino fell over himself after creating a good chance a couple of yards out, and then Quinn marginally mistimed the header off a cross by Ray Houghton.

Still, I can't really complain. We have got the result we came for, and if we made it a lot harder for ourselves than was absolutely necessary, it is a nice feeling to have started off our three-match programme with a win.

Our next World Cup game in Latvia is a fortnight away, and the players will now go home for a short break before reassembling in Dublin. In between, David O'Leary's testimonial game brings Hungary to Lansdowne Road, but essentially that fixture doesn't have any real relevance for us.

I thought for a time of keeping the players together in Ireland. But at the end of the day I decided against it. I did so on the basis that wives and girl-friends will be able to look after them better than I can, and in that I am almost certainly right!

9 · June · 1993

I got the call I always expected from Paul McGrath a couple of days ago. He told me that he was sorry for what had happened, promised not to repeat it, and asked if I would have him back. I told him I was happy to do so and promptly put him in the squad for the game against Latvia in Riga.

One of the great differences between your ordinary club team manager and a person like myself is that whereas the guy in charge of a club team can take disciplinary action against a player, I don't have that option.

The only punishment I can hand out is to decline to invite an individual back for our next match. But if he doesn't want to come in the first instance, that form of discipline doesn't amount to much.

Paul McGrath, I am certain, loves playing for Ireland; but his problem is that occasionally things can get too much for him, and instead of standing and facing a problem, he walks away. It transpired that his wife hadn't been too well at the time of the game in Albania. He felt that he was under pressure to play in that situation and decided that he couldn't handle it.

I talk a lot to Paul whilst he says very little to me. But if I ask him a question directly, he'll answer me politely, and when he travels, he's a smashing lad to have with you. Just occasionally, however, he wanders off, and when that happens I try to lead him back as gently as I can.

Part of a manager's brief is to take account of the different personalities in the squad and attempt to marry them in the collective group. That sounds very high fallutin', but it is a very real factor in man management.

Take Paul McGrath, for example. He's a loner, a guy who normally prefers his own company to anybody else's. He spends a lot of his free time in his room watching television, and more often than not he'll choose to eat on his own. He doesn't normally join in any of the leisure time activities organised for the squad, but that's his choice and I respect it!

Anyway, with McGrath back I don't have any problems picking my team. Some of the critics would have Kevin Moran in at centre-back in place of Alan Kernaghan, but in my book that was never a runner.

I've gone on record over and over again in saying that Kevin was one of Ireland's finest players, a superb competitor who never flinched in putting his head in positions in which others were loath to risk a boot. And as long as he stays that way, there will always be a strong case for picking him in the squad.

But the reality is that he's almost 37, more than ten years older than Kernaghan, and common sense demands that I play Alan. Kernaghan may still lack a little finesse, for want of a better word, in international football. But he's a good defender who is going to play a lot of important games for Ireland over a long period of time.

I suspect that factors other than football logic are at work in this particular case. The Irish public have never had any problems in identifying with lads born outside the country and cheering them on whenever they wear the green. But I'll tell you something: certain sections of the media are all hung up on the point.

To them, the ideal team would be one comprised of eleven home-grown players, preferably guys who have played hurling or

The home defeat by Spain was the most disappointing result of all the qualifying games. Still, there were good moments such as this when Niall Quinn won a high ball, despite the presence of three Spanish defenders.

The Irish team that drew 1-1 with Northern Ireland in Windsor Park in November 1993 to qualify for America.

Gaelic football at school, and then made good in English football. That, as far as it goes, is nice and idyllic, but unfortunately life is not quite as simple as that.

Frankly I get annoyed by all this talk about granny rules and the snide remarks about people calling in on boats at Portsmouth and qualifying for Ireland. That kind of talk doesn't wash with me and I have to say that a lot of it originates in England through envy.

We have built a good strong squad and without putting too fine a point on it, the English are jealous. Hence the derogatory remarks about ancestry and the rest. What they conveniently forget, of course, is that England have more 'dodgy' players in their squad than any of the other 'home' countries.

Every member of our squad has direct Irish lineage. Social circumstances and lack of work may have forced their parents to emigrate, but that doesn't make them any less Irish. There may be a whole range of accents to be heard in our dressing room, from Cockney to Scouse to Glaswegian. But don't try telling the owners that they're not Irish. I don't think they'd like it.

Before setting off for Riga, an Ireland selection played Hungary at Lansdowne Road in a testimonial game for David O'Leary. I have written before of the dangers of attaching too much importance to the friendly international fixtures, but a match like that against the Hungarians was even less credible.

It was simply a means of rewarding David O'Leary for his service to Ireland and I treated it as such. We started in great style with Roy Keane putting one away after just 30 seconds and Niall Quinn scoring a second shortly afterwards.

Then I started withdrawing players, thinning down the team too much and we ended up losing the game 4-2. It was a chastening reminder that once you start interfering with the engine of a team, anything can happen.

I had always rated the Latvians as the whipping boys for the other teams in the group, so I came here looking for a good win. With the ball holding up in the wind, they gave McGrath and Kernaghan a few problems early on. But once we settled, it was all done and dusted pretty quickly.

Denis Irwin provided a beauty of a cross for John Aldridge to head the first; and when Paul McGrath added a second before half-time, it could have been anything!

In our first meeting with Latvia at Lansdowne Road we scored four times – and we weren't flattered in doing so. Even though we were now playing them in their own backyard, I felt that we could repeat that achievement – and told the players as much in our half-time chat.

All the signs are that things are going to tighten at the top of the group, and if it comes down in the end to goal difference, I want to make certain that we're in there with a shout. This was a game in which we could do our goals difference column a lot of good, but we still had to exercise a certain amount of caution.

In many ways a two-goal lead, as we discovered in our European championship game in Poland, is the most dangerous of all. My dilemma now was: do I now tell my players to go out and chase more scores, and risk being caught out at the back in the process.

There is no doubt in my mind that if we get a third goal early in the second half, we'll destroy the Latvians. But unfortunately, from our point of view, the chances which might have pushed them over the top are wasted. And it's not all down to bad luck.

Time out of number we find huge gaps in their defence, but the final ball is just not good enough to produce goals, and on those occasions when we do get it right, we discover that somebody up there likes Latvia.

For example, a ball is played through for Andy Townsend just at the edge of the penalty area. It's on his favourite left foot and in those kinds of situations, my money will always be on Andy when he decides to let fly. Now he catches the ball just right, but the goalkeeper sticks out a hand in desperation, knocks it on to the crossbar and eventually it goes over.

When that sort of thing happens, you begin to worry. It's not that I felt we were going to lose the game, or even a point, but we were struggling to add to our two first-half goals. Try as we might, we just couldn't apply the final, decisive touch to a whole series of promising movements.

Roy Keane knocked one against a post! John Aldridge missed a couple from close in, and Steve Staunton also gaffed when he might have done better. It was all very frustrating, and when we got into the last quarter, I decided to reshuffle the pack in the hope that it might work the trick.

Before we got to that stage, I had taken off Niall Quinn and replaced him with Tony Cascarino. The previous night there was a scare story that Niall had suddenly been taken ill, and was going into hospital for an appendicitis operation.

The story was not true, but Niall did have a tummy upset which left him a little weakened. Despite that, he played his heart out as usual and had chased all over the park before I decided that he had nothing more to give, and sent on Cass. As it turned out, that was to lead me into a delicate and mildly embarrassing situation.

In our scheme of things the two central midfielders have a licence to get forward, but not at the same time. If Andy, for example, decides to make a run, it's up to Roy Keane to stay put and mind the shop. The reasons are pretty obvious, for if you leave a hole in midfield and your attacks break down, you are going to be punished on a counter-attack.

Now we've developed a little ploy which enables us to take account of this situation. We don't always use it, but just occasionally we take off one of our specialist strikers, send on an extra midfielder and thus allow both Keane and Townsend to run at the opposition without fear of being caught out. This, I decided, was one of those occasions when we needed to alter the pattern of the game; so I decided to send Ronnie Whelan and John Sheridan down behind the goal to warm up.

Keane had just injured himself by running into a post, and as he lay there on the grass, my mind was turning in a hundred different directions. At first I thought of substituting Tommy Coyne for Aldridge. I then favoured bringing in Whelan and Sheridan.

I told both players to strip, that I was bringing them on. Suddenly, I remembered that I had already used one of my substitutes. The trouble is that at this stage Sheridan and Whelan are both standing up just waiting for the nod to go on.

In normal circumstances I would probably have used Ronnie, but the problem now is that the UEFA man on the line already has John's number out and is holding it up, indicating that he is about to come on. How can I now tell Sheridan that I don't want him without insulting him in front of all those people?

So I tell Ronnie to go back into the dugout – and he sees red. Later in the evening, he has a go

The scoreboard that confirmed the result in Northern Ireland in Windsor Park in November 1993 to qualify for America.

 Captain Fantastic! Andy Townsend in action against Northern Ireland at Windsor Park.

 Terry Phelan and Maurice Setters celebrate at the end of the Windsor Park match.

at me in the hotel over the incident and I'm not impressed. He tells me that I've made him look like an idiot. I inform him that I make the team decisions without fear or favour of anybody.

Deep down I can, of course, appreciate what he is saying to me. Nobody likes to be put in a position like that, however unintentionally. But I was sincere at the particular time when I said that I had more to worry about than his bruised ego. It was an important game for everybody – him included – and the need to win took precedence over everything.

I'm not in the best of humour this evening. I realise I have made a mistake. And Ronnie knows it too.

Sadly the introduction of John Sheridan didn't have the desired effect in cracking the Latvian defence. Roy and Andy got into their penalty area so often that at times it seemed that we couldn't avoid putting another goal past them. But the scoreline stayed the same – and I stayed disappointed.

Funnily enough, the media and the people who watched the match on television seemed to be happy enough with the way it had gone. Like so much else in football, the result coloured everything and they were delighted that we had banked another two points.

I, too, was happy with the end product, even if I felt let down by our inability to put another couple in the net. We are coming to the end of a long, hard season, and while the spirit is willing, the flesh is beginning to weaken.

Still, it's funny how you can misread things. For example, I wasn't terribly impressed by Ray Houghton's performance and left the ground convinced that he, more than most, was beginning to suffer the physical legacies of a season that had simply gone on too long for him. It was only when I watched the video later that I discovered that he had winkled out the three best passes of the match. Those are the facts which can escape you in the heat of a game you desperately want to win.

When we leave for home tomorrow, it will be mission accomplished. We have achieved what we set out to achieve. Now only Lithuania in Vilnius stands between us and a perfect summer. Come hell or high water, I am determined that when we take our seasonal break, we will still be leading the Group Three table.

16 · June · 1993

To judge by the reaction of the media, there might have been only one player in our squad going to Lithuania. We may have some of the best footballers in Europe living in our team hotel, but as far as they are concerned there is only one person that is newsworthy – Roy Keane.

Now, I've never disguised my admiration for the player. He's skilful, he's competitive and he has one of the best engines I've ever seen in a young player. He'll start running for you from the kick-off, and 90 minutes later it's a pound to a penny that he'll be still motoring.

For all the big money in modern football, that kind of asset is still very precious and, as I said previously, it would have added significantly to our armoury if we had had him with us in Italy four years earlier.

Now young Roy was even more in demand. Brian Clough, the man who plucked him from the bread-and-butter world of Cobh Ramblers and built him into a huge attraction at Nottingham Forest, had just announced that he was quitting.

Moreover, Forest was relegated from the FA Premiership and with anything up to £4 million to be gained from selling Keane, they quickly made it clear that they were open to offers for him. Early on, Blackburn Rovers appeared to be the front runners for his signature, but gradually it transpired that Manchester United were also prepared to splash out big money for the young Cork man.

A funny crowd, the media. They ask the same question of the young man, day after day. Is it to be Blackburn or United? And over and over again he tells them that he hasn't reached a decision. But is that the end of it? Not on your life. And so the ritual goes on.

In fairness, they are not the only players in this particular cameo. I have various managers ringing me up from England asking me about Roy, and I tell them that it has nothing to do with me. After all, I have just borrowed him from his club and the last thing I want to be seen to be doing is influencing his choice of a new club.

I was, however, genuinely worried that all this rumour-mongering would upset the lad. Here we were preparing for a vital game that can play a big part in determining whether we go to the World Cup finals, and one of our key players was being pestered with enquiries about things which had no direct relevance to the job in hand.

So I called the lad into my room and advised him to try and put all this talk about a transfer to the back of his mind and concentrate on our game. The offers, I told him, would still be there when we got back and then he could deal with them in his own good time.

Roy, to his credit, showed a lot of maturity in the way he handled the situation. It wasn't his fault that the phones were hopping mad. But he took it all in his stride and, despite the pressures, he trained as hard as the others when we went to work.

The preparatory work in this instance was undertaken at Carrickmacross in Co. Monaghan. It was recommended that we stay in the Nuremore Hotel there, and I have to say that it was an excellent choice. Normally we set up camp for our home games at the International Airport Hotel in Dublin where we are looked after extremely well. As far as I know, it is our intention to stay there for the ordinary international games; but on those occasions when we are together for a week or more, a place like the Nuremore is ideal.

There is a golf course adjoining the hotel, fishing facilities are also available near by, and for those who like to walk, there is no better place. One way or another it was an ideal location for us as we found ourselves with time to kill between the game against Latvia the previous week and our visit to Lithuania.

For a while I had thought about telling the players to go back home for a couple of days, but decided against it. I realised better than most just how long and difficult the season had been for them. But after weighing the pros and cons, I reckoned that it would be better to keep them together for one last final push.

We had done extremely well to get maximum points from our games in Albania and Latvia. The last thing I wanted was to put our position at risk by getting it wrong in the build-up to Lithuania.

Niall Quinn and Alan McDonald challenge for the ball in Windsor Park.

Two shots of John Aldridge and Alan McDonald in the 1-1 draw at Windsor Park.

We travelled to Carrickmacross directly on our return from Riga, and I told the players that the next two days would be 'fun' days. They could do anything they liked, within reason, but come Sunday morning, it was back to business as usual.

As it transpired, the highlight of the leisure programme was a golfing competition in which I participated on Saturday. I'm not sure who won it in the end, but I suspect that there were a couple of dodgy scores returned by a couple of interested parties. Still, it was all good fun and though not a regular golfer, I enjoyed it immensely.

At one point, I had thought about going back home briefly on the Thursday. My daughter Debbie was going on holiday with her two children, Emma and Christopher, the following day, and since I hadn't seen them for a couple of weeks, I figured it would be a good idea to have a chat before they took off on their break.

In fact, I didn't go. Much as I fancied the idea, I reckoned it would be unfair to return home at a time when the players were being asked to make the sacrifice of staying in camp. The exception was David O'Leary, who came to me in Latvia and asked if he could go to Leeds to discuss the details of his transfer with Howard Wilkinson.

I had no hesitation in agreeing, and it is a measure of David's gratitude that he drove through the night from Leeds in order to catch an early flight out of London and was back in Carrickmacross on Saturday morning.

Ironically, we were still one player light on the Saturday, for Eddie McGoldrick came to me in my room and asked permission to return to London to sign for Arsenal. As far as I was concerned, that approach by Arsenal was unexpected, but I was delighted for Eddie. He had come on like the proverbial ton since playing his first game for us, and in a situation in which George Graham needed a utility player who could, among other things, fill in for the departed O'Leary, he couldn't have chosen better. Eddie duly signed for Arsenal for a reported fee of £1 million and I was delighted for him.

Training, as planned, began in earnest on Sunday morning and I was amazed by the number of people who turned up to watch us. There must have been between 3,000 and 5,000 people present at the first session and that was a real eye opener for everybody.

It showed once more how the team has captured the imagination of the Irish public, and even if it meant a delayed departure back to the hotel as the Gardaí sought to clear the way for us, it was still great to see. When we eventually left Co. Monaghan on Tuesday morning, it was with genuine reluctance.

Picking the team caused me no problems at all. There were still those who wanted Kevin Moran in place of Alan Kernaghan at centre-back. But that was never going to happen. Niall Quinn had fully recovered from the tummy bug which had affected him in Riga, and in that situation he again kept the target-man job to the exclusion of Tony Cascarino.

If the selection of our team was a mere formality, I was a little worried by conflicting reports about the make-up of the Lithuanian team. I had seen them play three times and without question they were the best of the less fancied teams in Group Three.

Now some of the Irish journalists were telling me that the Lithuanian Federation authorities were unable to come up with the cash to pay the insurance premiums for their western-based players and that FC Vienna were refusing to release three of their players for the game.

In support of this, they showed me fax messages purporting to come from the Lithuanian Federation. Even so, I doubted their authenticity. Certainly, those players whom I had marked down as their best were all present and correct when the teams came out on to the pitch.

On the way to Vilnius, somebody mentioned that no Irish team had ever won three games on the trot away from home. That did nothing to ease the sense of foreboding as the players got their last-minute instructions and we pushed them out through the door of the dressing room.

In many respects, the start of the game was not dissimilar from that in Latvia. There was a lot of tension in our players and it showed – particularly at the back where we looked very nervy in the early stages.

Gradually, however, we settled in and in the 40th minute we got the vital break and the only goal of the game. Roy Keane was fouled just outside the box, and when Steve Staunton drove the free kick in low, it skidded off the boot of Baltusnikas into the corner of the net.

Steve was adamant that it would have gone in anyway and, of course, we were only too willing to believe him. Interestingly, two of our three previous World Cup goals also originated from set pieces which merely strengthened a theory I hold. Despite the sophistication of the blackboard game, modern football has evolved in such a manner that more and more goals are coming from dead ball situations. In those circumstances, I'm very glad that we have two such precise strikers of the ball as Staunton and Irwin in our team.

That Baltusnikas should have the misfortune

to deflect the ball into his own net was vaguely ironic for, undoubtedly, he was their most active player and was involved in almost everything that mattered for Lithuania.

Before the goal, for instance, he had popped up on the line to clear after Roy Keane's shot had beaten the goalkeeper; and then he was involved in a hair-raising incident from our point of view when he drove a forty yard free kick low against a post, with Bonner beaten to the world.

That, I have to admit, was a real let-off for us. But had it gone in, it still would have been a gross injustice. We were far and away the better team, particularly in the second half when Staunton and Aldridge missed good chances of polishing the scoreline.

Still, it was great to win the game and succeed in what we had set out to achieve. We have collected six points from our end of season programme. Now, America beckons. Barring a catastrophe, I am pretty certain that these three wins will qualify us for the finals.

Only two things annoyed me. One was a second booking for Paul McGrath after he had deliberately pulled down an opponent approaching half-time. Then, literally, thirty seconds before the finish, Ray Houghton was shown a yellow card for something I didn't quite see. Ray and Steve were standing over the ball after we had been awarded a free kick when suddenly the referee, Roger Phillipi of Luxemburg, reached into his back pocket for a card.

Incensed, I make for the referee as he is walking off the field and ask, 'Can I have a word, please?' Bitter experience has taught me that this is the best way to approach match officials in such situations. I ask why he's booked Houghton.

He tells me it's because he took the free too

quickly and that only makes me madder. I ask him if he'd prefer us to have wasted time and, sheepishly, he informs me that he is only applying the law. And I secretly curse those stupid people who dream up legislation like that.

Then, I turn my anger on Houghton as we're walking off the pitch and he, rightly, has a go back at me. He tells me that he is not in the habit of picking up yellow cards and if I have a gripe, I should go and see the referee. And, of course, he was dead right.

That puts me in one of my little moods and when RTE come to me for a post-match interview, I refuse. I've been threatening to do that for some time, for these people are taking me for granted and trading off my good-will. After all, I too am a professional and if I work for them, I expect to be paid. But eventually I relent and talk with George Hamilton.

It was a shame that I had to go bitching like that at the end of what ought to have been a very happy day. But it's been a nervy time, these last three matches. I'm feeling it inside. We all need a holiday. I'm going fishing.

7 · September · 1993

It's back to the coal face again after the summer break. It's true what they say: time flies even faster as you get older. It seems like no time at all since we were jetting back from Vilnius, delighted to have achieved our third away win in as many games, and looking forward to a long summer break.

Now it's time to do battle with the Lithuanians for a second time. We're into the home stretch.

Students of mathematics tell me that if we beat Lithuania at Lansdowne tomorrow, we need just one point from either of our last two fixtures against Spain in Dublin and Northern Ireland in Belfast to qualify. This is, indeed, a possibility, but I'm looking for a minimum of four points from those three matches, just to be certain.

Almost certainly the Lithuanian game will be less difficult to win than either of the last two, but that still doesn't make it a formality, not by a long stretch. Even though they're playing just for pride, they'll be difficult enough to crack –

particularly if they are given a chance to settle at the back!

As I said, the summer weeks have flown and I'm reminded yet again of how long the old season lasted. Mick Byrne counts the hamstring casualties and tells me that Andy Townsend, Kevin Moran and Niall Quinn are all having problems with this particular injury. I'm not just speaking with the benefit of hindsight when I say that I predicted this kind of trouble when the new season began.

It was 20 June when our players packed up for the season. Then it was two or three weeks holidays, and before they knew it, they were back in pre-season training. That kind of break is far too short, and the tell-tale sign of a player having problems in readjusting too quickly is the damaged hamstring.

Professional players who have been soldiering for ten or eleven months need a longer break than that, and if they don't get it they are in danger of cracking up. I remember back in 1970,

Eddie McGoldrick (above) and Niall Quinn making a tackle (below) were two of the Republic of Ireland's stars in the tension-filled draw against Northern Ireland at Windsor Park.

after being to the World Cup finals with England, experiencing one of the roughest periods of my career when the new season started.

Like the Irish players I now manage, I simply hadn't a chance of resting my body sufficiently and after 'doing' my hamstring in a pre-season game up at Celtic, I was out of football for a long time.

Just because players are paid handsomely in the modern game, people expect them to perform like machines. The level of fitness required to survive at the top level is now frightening, and there are some who are beginning to ask serious questions about the demands being made on those involved.

Nor were those tweaking hamstrings the only problems on our horizons. I got a call from Manchester City to say that Terry Phelan was in bed with tonsillitis and would struggle to make the game in Dublin.

Tommy Coyne, whose wife had died tragically during the summer, is unavailable and that is perfectly understandable. I told him to look after his personal affairs, forget about football for a time and that we'd talk later.

Missing also is David O'Leary whose close season move from Arsenal to Leeds United had ended one of the great club-player relationships in English football. Unfortunately, his early days at Elland Road did not go as smoothly as expected, and after picking up a pre-season injury, he is unavailable to us for the Lithuanian match. Coupled with a one-match ban on Paul McGrath, who had been booked for a second time in Vilnius, and Kevin Moran's nagging injury, it leaves us with a real problem in the centre of our defence. What a contrast that makes to the days when we were top heavy with options in those positions!

Alan Kernaghan is, of course, available and I was grateful for that. Finding an alternative partner for him was not quite so easy. At one stage I even gave some thought to the idea of dropping Roy Keane back into the defence and bringing Ronnie Whelan into midfield.

It was reassuring to have Ronnie on stand-by, and Roy had shown on occasions with Notts Forest that he was capable of doing the sweeper job to perfection. Eventually I discarded the idea on the basis that it would be outrageous to waste such a talent in defence. But in any event, Kevin Moran's recovery ensured that I didn't have to make that choice.

Andy Townsend, too, proved his fitness when playing for Aston Villa against Everton last Tuesday, and with Phelan checking in on schedule at the team hotel, it means that our injury problems aren't nearly as bad as had been imagined.

Unfortunately, the earlier uncertainty left its scars to some degree and in the eight-a-side match in training on Tuesday, I discovered that many players were holding back. Normally, these sessions are fiercely competitive but, now conscious of the earlier injuries, I had instructed them to be careful with their tackles.

And that was only half the story. Back in the hotel, I was preaching to them about the need to be careful with the referee.

Six of our players have yellow cards. The last thing I want are more bookings – bookings which would put them out of the crucial match with Spain.

Then again, I was after them about the need to be vigilant in defence. The Lithuanians, I felt, could be dangerous on the break, and we couldn't afford to leave any gaps for them to indulge their pace through the middle.

8 · September · 1993

One way or another, I seem to have been more negative than positive in my team talks and in my heart of hearts I knew that was wrong. You can't send people out to play a vital World Cup game with a litany of don'ts ringing in their ears – and yet here I was, doing just that. It all added up to the unmistakable signs of pressure.

It was a tough afternoon at Lansdowne today. Just as they had done in Vilnius, the Lithuanians showed themselves to be strong, athletic players who spared nothing or nobody on the day. And the irony was that they did to us what we had done to others so often in the past.

They closed us down every time we had the ball, got in behind us on the rare occasions they pushed forward, and generally showed the benefits of a team which had done its homework. Coupled with our own inhibitions, it made for a long, tense afternoon.

There have been many occasions in the past when we suffered in the wait for a lead goal, but that was certainly not the case today. In fact, the game was only four minutes in progress when the Lithuanian goalkeeper, Gintaras Stance, was retrieving the ball from his net.

Steve Staunton created the chance with a low, driven cross into the six yard area, and John Aldridge read it perfectly to race in and put it away from just a couple of yards. That ought to have provided the platform for a big win, but unfortunately it didn't work out quite like that.

Before the game, we identified Virginijus Baltusnikas as a possible weak link in the Lithuanian team. It was his own goal, if you recall, which gave us victory in Vilnius and that, I felt, was no mere fluke.

Baltusnikas fancied himself as a sweeper who could play a bit. Our plan was to encourage him in that belief and then, when he had the ball, put him under a lot of pressure. I reckon we were right in our thinking, but unfortunately the chances which could have done our goal difference a lot of good were squandered to the disappointment of the crowd and the dismay of the rest of us on the bench.

Kevin Moran knocked one against a post, Staunton went close on a couple of occasions, and Ray Houghton wrote a fitting postscript to it all when he missed a sitter shortly before the finish. In the end, we were grateful for Alan Kernaghan's goal, his first for Ireland, which effectively wrapped up the game for us before half-time.

Denis Irwin, dependable as ever, was one of our better players on the day, and he duly provided the cross from which Kernaghan, on the burst, made the glancing header and the ball ended in the net. Alan was of course delighted, but the predominant feeling among the rest of us was one of relief.

It was not one of our best days, basically because we were too inhibited. But a win is a win and the 2-0 scoreline would be noted all round Europe before the big evening programme got under way.

One of the early kick-offs was in Tirana, where Denmark met Albania in a game with profound implications for every team in the group. The Danes were on a bit of a run and everybody in Europe, I reckoned, expected them

The end of the Northern Ireland match in Windsor Park was one of the tensest, yet happy occasions during my time as manager. Talking to the press (right). Andy Townsend and Mick Byrne celebrate (below).

The unfortunate altercation between Billy Bingham and myself (left). Happy with a job well done (below).

to win with some ease against the bottom placed team in Group Three.

But I had seen enough in our match in Tirana to convince me that if the Albanians brought all their players back for the Danish fixture and if the ball ran kindly for them, they might just do us a favour by taking a point from the European champions.

In fact, when we got back to the dressing room, Mick Byrne came up to me and was so excited that he couldn't get the words out. 'Boss', he says, 'I've just heard that Albania have won 1-0 – and its official!'

My initial reaction to that was one of suspicion. The Danes, I told him, had too many class players at their disposal to bite the dust in Albania and I wouldn't believe it until I saw the evidence with my own eyes. I could scarcely wait to get back to our hotel to start checking things out. Sadly, I discovered that my gut reaction was right. The result we had been given referred to an Under-21 game – the Danes had won the senior match again by a 1-0 margin.

Frank Pingel got the all important goal after 63 minutes and Richard Moeller Nielsen, the Danish manager, said that if the Albanians played like this when Spain arrived in Tirana on 22 September, they were in with a chance of beating them. I only hope that he is right

This evening I've skipped the celebrations. Instead, I'm staying in to watch England on the box against Poland at Wembley. It's a game they cannot afford to lose, and as I've already made clear, I'm hoping against hope that they'll survive.

The honeymoon is long since over for Graham Taylor, and I can only guess at his innermost thoughts as he leads his team out. They started shakily enough, and even after Les Ferdinand had given them the lead, they still struggled to impose their class on the game.

To make matters worse, Paul Gascoigne has gone and got himself booked for a second time and is now out of the crunch meeting with Holland in Rotterdam, a game which may well determine their chances of going to the finals.

It's at times like this that people get infuriated with Gazza but then, right on cue, he puts the record straight with a glorious goal, and before the end Stuart Pearce rifled a free kick into the roof of the net to put a better gloss on England's night.

No less than myself, Graham Taylor realises that he still has a lot of work ahead of him before the big cut is made; but this win polished by some excellent football in the second half will put him in better heart for that Dutch assignment.

6 · October · 1993

From a long way back, this was going to be the big one.

It was, of course, essential that we won our three away games at the end of the season. And despite what others thought, I was happy to walk away from Lansdowne and bank two more points from the home match with Lithuania.

But the return leg of the Spanish game was always going to be something else. The days when the Spaniards were regarded as brittle travellers are long gone. They've adapted their game to meet their needs. They're going to be a huge test for us – even in Dublin.

They knew they were lucky to take a point from us in Seville. That was more than they deserved on the day, but Javier Clemente, shrewd man that he is, will be looking at the video of that game and wondering how he can now turn it to his advantage.

Even if we fail to do the business against the Spaniards, we can still qualify by beating Northern Ireland in our last game at Windsor Park. But I've never fancied the idea of having to go to Belfast looking for a 'result'. Far better to get it done and dusted at Lansdowne Road; and besides, I've always subscribed to the old maxim of never putting off until tomorrow what can be done today.

Therefore this is a huge game for us, but I'm just a little worried by some of the vibes coming back from Dublin. The feeling over there is that this is a game like no other and that the whole country is going to be tuned into it. Given the fact that it can decide whether or not we go to the finals, I can well understand the buzz of excitement, but what worries me deeply is the apparent expectation of the Irish people that we're somehow going to clobber the Spaniards.

I hope and believe we'll win this game, but clobber the Spaniards? Never. The way they play their football they're never going to be badly beaten home or away. I think that they'll come to Dublin looking for a point. They'll pack their defence and bank on catching us on the break, and in that situation I'll be amazed if we beat them easily.

My first priority is to ensure that we get at least a point out of the game. But as I've explained before, I'm really after the win that will wrap up qualification for us. As far as I'm concerned, I want Christmas to arrive in October.

That said, the early vibes are not encouraging. Andy Townsend did his hamstring last week and Ron Atkinson has been on the phone to tell me that there's no chance of the player joining us in Dublin. I don't have to stress how serious the blow is and how it has changed my thinking on the game. At this stage, I think I can cope with most team situations, but when you start tinkering about with the engine of the side, you're into potential trouble.

Together with Roy Keane, Andy forms the engine of our side – a strong aggressive runner who, in addition to skippering the team, is largely responsible for anchoring the midfield.

To make matters worse, I've had word from Tranmere that John Aldridge is still struggling with a dodgy hamstring. He's missed three club games already and Johnny King, the Tranmere manager, tells me that there's a big doubt if Aldo will play against Bolton next Saturday.

Even if he misses that one, however, I reckon that the extra day's rest will see him right for this day week, and John tells me as much when I speak with him on the phone.

11 · October · 1993

I was at home on Friday when the phone rang and Johnny King told me that Aldo has suffered a reaction in training. He pulled him out of the Bolton game, but decent man that he is, he will allow John to come and join us.

On Saturday, I thought that he'd be ready by Wednesday. But then something remarkable happened. Aldo went home and without any medical advice put a poultice on the injured part of his leg. Now poultices are dangerous things as anybody will tell you – particularly when they're not properly tested before being applied.

But Aldo, with scant regard for his health, goes home and without taking any precautions, straps one on his leg. The end product is that he scalds a part of his leg and far from improving things, he's merely gone and aggravated the situation. When he eventually joined us today, I knew immediately that he had no chance of making it. But I cannot let the Spaniards know that – at least not yet.

It means that we must now go into the game without two players – and that changes everything. Once I knew that Townsend was out, I was determined that I would bring in Ronnie Whelan in a straight swap in midfield. But now with Aldo also gone, the game plan has to be revised more drastically.

Instinct tells me that in a situation in which the Spaniards would seek to take some of the pace out of the game by pushing the ball about at the back, I needed two front people to put them under pressure. John, in tandem with Niall Quinn, does that job superbly; but now that he was out, I didn't have an adequate replacement

and I have to gamble.

On different occasions over the years, I had gone with an extra midfielder and played only one specialist forward. This, I figure, is one of those occasions when circumstances dictated tactics and the gamble justified the risk. With Spain certain to clutter up the middle of their defence with bodies, the best way is to go round them rather than through them.

It is, of course, a gamble, but having thought long and hard about David Kelly, the only other front runner in the squad, I reckon it would be wiser to go with just Niall Quinn up front and depend on the wide players, Denis Irwin, Ray Houghton, Terry Phelan and Steve Staunton to provide the chances for Quinn or perhaps Roy Keane to exploit.

Ronnie Whelan and Paul McGrath will anchor midfield and prevent Spain getting at our back four on the break. At this stage of his career Ronnie is not the quickest player around, but he's vastly experienced and knows how to stop people from playing.

13 · October · 1993

I kept up the pretence about Aldo right to the end, even to the point of putting a No. 10 shirt on him as the players assembled outside the dressing rooms. That caused a bit of a flutter among the Spaniards, who by now guessed that there was something wrong with John, but of course we couldn't keep the ruse going indefinitely.

In all my years in football, I had never known a more expectant atmosphere at a game. A huge explosion of sound greeted the teams when they came out, the stadium fairly cracked with excitement, and nobody could be in any doubt

that this was, indeed, something special.

We started promisingly enough, knocking the ball about in confident fashion and had already put together a couple of promising moves, when the roof fell in on us after only 12 minutes. As in the way of these things, it started innocently enough with Alan Kernaghan coming across to knock the ball into touch.

What happened next was interesting. Alan appeared to run over the touch line, did a little half-circle before running back on to the pitch. The result was that he was not in the textbook position when the ball was thrown to Julio Salinas.

The only other Spaniard in the penalty area, as far as I could see, was Jose Caminero. But yes, you've guessed. Salinas somehow finds him with the header and the lad hits a glorious volley into the roof of the net. The obvious thing is to say that there is no legislating for something like that. When it happens it happens, and you just grin and bear it. But I don't agree.

For one thing, there ought to have been somebody jumping with Salinas and putting him under pressure. And it baffles me how Caminero was able to get a clear shot at the target. Kevin Moran, as I recall, was standing close to him, but instead of trying to head the ball out of danger, he tried to kick it and was beaten to the bounce by Caminero.

In my wildest dreams I had never imagined Spain scoring so early – and I bet neither did they. And that sadly, is only the beginning of our troubles. I'm standing there recalling the build-up to that goal when suddenly we're two down. Kevin Moran is pushing up to play offside when the ball is played through quickly for Salinas to chase.

Kernaghan spots the danger, cuts across, and doing everything right he gets goalside of the Spaniard. He appears to have the situation under control as the two of them race to the end line, but for some reason best known to himself, he declines to knock the ball out for a corner when they arrive at the end line.

Instead, he somehow manages to fall over himself, allowing Salinas to drag the ball back. Even then the danger is not all that great, for there isn't a Spaniard around to take a pass from him. So, taking the only option open to him, he goes for the tiny space between Packie Bonner and the post and the ball incredibly ends in the net off Packie's boot.

I've just seen the ball in our net on two occasions, and yet I can't believe it. This can't be the game that Javier Clemente and I planned for. In his case, Christmas has come early. In mine, it's a bloody nightmare!

The Spaniards have got into our penalty area just twice, never pushed more than two players forward at any time, and yet we're two goals down after just 16 minutes. It's too bad to be real from my point of view. And when Kernaghan thumped a header against the crossbar shortly afterwards, I know for sure that it's not going to be our day.

To make matters worse, Kevin Moran has gone and 'done' his groin; and even as I'm watching Moran, Mick Byrne tells me that Steve Staunton is also in trouble. Kevin has to be replaced immediately. The question is by whom, and in what formation.

At 2-0 down we're in a desperate situation. I've only got one specialist forward, Tony Cascarino, on the bench and I've got to decide the best time to bring him in. Normally, I would leave it until 20 minutes from the end, but obviously, that is not now practical. Eventually – and in this I'm influenced by Staunton's problems – I replace Kevin with a midfielder, John Sheridan, and resolve to wait until the second half, when we will have the wind behind us, to introduce Cass.

Sheridan, as it turns out, is a wise choice. Even with so much going wrong around him, he has a fine game, but typical of our luck on the day, he pays a cruel price for his only mistake in the twenty-sixth minute.

The Spaniards, quickly down the right, and John doing everything right tracks back to cover it. Unfortunately, he's so intent on getting a boot to the ball that he fails to see Denis Irwin on his

Gary Kelly and Bryan Roy tussle for the ball in our great 1-0 win against Holland on 20 April. A boy's-eye view of some of our lads.

left coming across to clear. The upshot is that John, in attempting to flykick to safety, sends it to the only Spaniard in the vicinity of our penalty area, and Julio Salinas doesn't spurn gifts like that.

Now we're three down and the sense of disbelief is everywhere. Everything we didn't want to happen has happened. Every dream of glory has been broken. When we get into the dressing room at half-time, there's no ranting or raving, only a deep sense of numbed shock. In any event, there are so many injury problems, that I don't have time to talk.

It is clear that Staunton can't go back out in the second half, so I put on Cascarino and revert to a 4-4-2 formation. But Denis Irwin is now carrying a dead leg, and in normal circumstances would have been replaced. But given that we've already used our two substitutes he has to soldier on.

With Staunton gone I've got no left-side

player in midfield. Ronnie Whelan has played there for Liverpool and he tells me that he is ready to do the job again, in the hope of knocking a few balls in with his right foot.

As it transpires we get a lot of crosses in from the flanks, but the breaks we're looking for just won't come. Niall Quinn's back header from a cross by Paul McGrath has the Spanish 'keeper Zubizarreta beaten all ends up, but just goes a couple of inches the wrong side of the post.

Eventually, we get a goal back when Sheridan slots one from short range and hope, faint hope, surfaces again. But sadly it's a case of too little, too late, and when Cascarino sees his header taken off the line in injury time, it somehow sums up the whole unhappy day.

I've known some disillusioning days in my time, but as I sit in the coach taking us back to the team hotel, I figure this has to be right up there at the top of the list. Awful! Bloody awful!

16 · October · 1993

I open my paper to discover that even before England are eliminated from the World Cup, there are people calling for Graham Taylor's head and demanding that he should resign.

In the aftermath of their 2-0 defeat by Holland at Rotterdam, it looks, indeed, as if England are gone. They can still scrape in by the back door by scoring something like eight or nine goals in their last game against San Marino and then depend on Poland doing the business against the Dutch. But that looks unlikely.

Knowing Graham Taylor, I fully expect him to resign before he is pushed, but to start calling for his dismissal even before they are mathematically dead is stretching things too

much. And once again it calls into question the priorities of a section of the English tabloid press.

Do they really want England to qualify for the finals or are they more interested in 'gutting' the person with the job of selecting the team. Sometimes I stand back from the situation, ask the question aloud and come up with the second scenario as the most likely answer.

Graham Taylor is an honest man who is doing the job to the best of his ability. But I wonder do the critics who berate him ever stop to consider the circumstances, over which he has no control, which contrive to shape the success or failure of his mission.

Take the game in Rotterdam the other night. I thought England did very well in an extremely trying situation in the first half, and at 0-0 they were well in there with a chance of achieving the result which would revive their hopes of qualification.

Then, in the space of a few dramatic seconds, the shape of the game changed. David Platt, doing everything right, got in behind the Dutch defence, and was streaking for goal when he was literally pulled from behind by Ronald Koeman.

In the kind of situation in which Platt found himself, my money would have been on him to go and finish the job, and Koeman, caught for pace, also sensed the worst when David reached the penalty area.

Like the shrewd professional that he is, he risked the foul and gambled on the referee's charity. In that, his judgment proved absolutely faultless.

To most of us watching on television, it seemed that the foul had taken place inside the penalty area. But as soon as the referee blew, Koeman, sensing his indecision, pointed to a spot just outside the area. After looking at his linesman the referee agreed with the Dutchman, and instead of a penalty awarded a free kick.

That, for my money, was a grave miscarriage of justice. But, of course, it was only half the story. Koeman had been guilty of the most cynical professional foul, and according to the book he should have 'walked' for it. Instead of the red card, however, the referee showed him a yellow one and our friend Ronald was the first to acknowledge that he had just got out of jail.

Unfortunately, for England, the cost of that decision by the referee was to be uncommonly high. Shortly afterwards, the Dutch got a free kick just outside the box, and Koeman, who by that stage ought to have been back in the dressing room, curled it into the net for the goal

which effectively cost Graham Taylor his job.

To any fair-minded person that was grossly unfair and it illustrated yet again the lottery by which a manager, any manager, can have his work brought to nothing by a couple of bizarre refereeing decisions. And I had reason to appreciate that better than most.

Cast your mind back almost a year to the night we played Spain in Seville. In an identical incident to the Koeman-Platt affair, John Aldridge was clear in Seville until he was chopped by the Spanish central defender.

In fairness to the referee on that occasion, he had no hesitation in giving the Spaniard his marching orders; but frankly I would have preferred it if he had given us the penalty kick, to which I felt we were entitled, rather than the free kick at the edge of the penalty area.

Then of course there was the incident later in the game when John Aldridge took the ball around the goalkeeper, placed it in the empty net and then looked up to see a linesman flagging for offside. Even after almost a year, that was an outrageous decision which has contrived to distort the whole group.

We're all entitled to make the occasional mistake and match officials are no different to anybody else. But did the tabloid critics take that into account when they rushed to condemn Taylor? Not likely!

There are a lot of people around who will sneer if England fail to make the cut for America, but don't number me among that lot. After all, I am English. I was born in the country and I was lucky enough to follow my uncle Jack and our kid, Bobby, into the England team. No, I want to see them go to the States as qualifiers; but in saying that, I must confess a vested interest.

The Irish win against Germany in Hanover on 29 May was one of the best results in our history. Andy Townsend (above) captained the team superbly to what was a famous victory.

As long as England is involved, it will take the limelight off us and shield us from the kind of publicity that Graham and, before him, Bobby Robson had to endure. If the English fail to make it, then I fear we'll become the target for the British press and that could change things totally.

The sad thing is that if they are eliminated, Taylor will carry the can and the FA officials at Lancaster Gate will go blithely on their way as if they had no hand, act or part in that failure. But that, of course, is utter rubbish.

I've said many, many times in the past that the domestic game in Britain needs to be restructured, and that the people who run the show in England must decide whether they want to oversee what they view as the best league championship in the world, or whether they wish to contribute significantly to a situation in which England will one day be back on top of the international ratings.

That, I believe, is the stark choice confronting them. There is no fudging the issue, no retreating to a situation in which all the blame is heaped on the unfortunate manager of the team. The problem is that the top players in England are asked to play too many times and very often are leg-weary for vital international games.

The clubs claim that if they pay these people big money, they must recoup that outlay by arranging more and more games. And so the catch-22 scenario goes on, compounded by the demands of people whose interest in the national team does not extend beyond a cursory glance at the paper.

As a concession to the national team manager

of England, the authorities have in comparatively recent times agreed to cancel the Premiership games immediately before a big international fixture. That is a step in the right direction, but it doesn't altogether address the fundamental issue of rationalising a club programme which, frankly, has become top heavy.

Graham Taylor is a man with a proven track record in football. At club level he was one of the most astute managers around, and no less than Bobby Robson, he seemed the right man at the right time for England.

Bobby, I'm sure, could have told him a thing or two about the perils of the trade, but being the man he is, Graham preferred to tackle them in his own individual way. As of now it doesn't look as if he is going to succeed. But again, I blame the system.

At the end of the article foreshadowing Graham's departure is a list of the main contenders to succeed him. And there, right at the end of it, is the name Jack Charlton.

Now it's common knowledge that I once applied for the job of managing the England team and didn't even get a reply from the FA. It's also pretty well known, I think, that I regard that rejection as one of my luckier breaks in football.

So why in heaven's name would I want the job now when I'm twelve years older and still at odds with a system which I believe works unfairly against the national team manager?

Besides, I've still got an important job to do for the Republic of Ireland. And part of that brief is to take them to the World Cup finals in the United States next summer.

17 · November · 1993

Northern Ireland in Belfast will never be easy pickings for a team from the south, but this was something else. As I've mentioned before, I desperately wanted to have our place in the World Cup finals secured before we played at Windsor Park. Circumstances contrived to ruin that ambition, and we suffered for it.

For one thing, I didn't realise how hurt Billy Bingham was by that defeat in Dublin earlier in the year. He didn't show it at the time, but I know now that he was deeply affected by the 3-0 scoreline.

He announced some time ago that he intended to quit as manager of the team after this game, and that, coupled with the Dublin experience, made him even more determined than usual to put one over on us.

As a manager, I could appreciate that kind of motivation. What I couldn't understand was his reference to our players as 'carpetbaggers'. He'd never said it before, at least not publicly, and I wondered about the timing of it now.

If Billy was hurt by the hammering we gave them at Lansdowne, I was saddened by that remark. These were my players he was talking about, and I was not going to have them talked down by anybody. I pointed out to him that all my players were Irish, if not all native born, and that in selecting them for my squad I was acting within the rules of FIFA. If Billy Bingham or anybody else doubted that, let them take the matter up with the appropriate authorities in Switzerland.

The other inflammatory factor in the build-up to the game was the speculation in the press that it might be taken out of Belfast and played in either England or mainland Europe. Even by Northern Ireland standards, the weeks before the game were particularly bad in terms of killings and violence, with one atrocity following another.

In that situation, there were genuine fears that this meeting of the two Ireland teams posed an unacceptable threat to law and order, and that it would be wiser to site it somewhere else. The Northern Ireland people were offended by that attitude, and made it clear to FIFA that the match stayed at Windsor Park. Our role in the matter was purely peripheral. We would play anywhere we were told to play, and if the fixture stayed in Belfast, so be it.

Conscious of the need to concentrate minds, I decided to bring the players to Ireland two days ahead of normal, on Friday, and instead of staying in Dublin, we based ourselves in the Nuremore Hotel in Co. Monaghan, where we had been looked after so well in the summer.

I felt we needed time to be alone to work on aspects of our game which had gone a bit rusty. And top of the list was the need to sharpen our finish in and around the penalty area. Instead of snatching at chances, I wanted players to take that extra second to compose themselves before delivering the shot. If they did, I felt the rewards could be significant.

Before we ever got to Monaghan, however, I had lost six players from the original squad. Steve Staunton, Ronnie Whelan, John Sheridan, Chris Morris, Kevin Sheedy and Kevin Moran were all ruled out because of injuries. Of these Staunton was unquestionably the biggest loss.

The scoreboard in Hanover tells it all (above) while Tony Cascarino celebrates the opening goal against Germany (below).

Niedersachsenstadion Hannover

Länderspiel

Deutschland 0

Irland 2

Mercedes-Benz

We've never been spoiled for choice in his position on the left side of midfield, and with Whelan and Sheedy both unavailable, I knew that we would struggle to replace Staunton. Eventually, I decided I would go with Eddie McGoldrick, who had played there in an emergency role in the game in Denmark a year earlier.

Eddie is a natural right-sided player, but thanks to his days at Crystal Palace where he was required to play in a whole range of roles, he is a very adaptable lad who is the answer to every manager's prayer. This was going to be a game for men, but in spite of his relative inexperience, I know he can handle it.

Despite all the withdrawals, the structure of the side remained largely intact, if one excepted the loss of Staunton; but I was just a little concerned that if changes became necessary, I didn't have a lot of options going for me.

The game itself wasn't long in progress when I discovered that much of what we had worked on in Monaghan was useless. I had preached to them the value of not rushing things, of taking a quick look to see what was on, of getting settled before striking the ball. And yet here they were doing precisely the opposite on a night when we needed to have all our wits about us.

Mind you, we had some good positions in the first half; but instead of receiving the ball, taking some of the pace off it and then having a 'dig' at goal, we were trying to do things at a hundred miles an hour.

Then again, people like Niall Quinn, John Aldridge and Ray Houghton were guilty of over-doing the little one-twos in the hope of getting somebody free at the end. That annoyed me – and so did the quality of the crossing. Even good crossers of the ball like Denis Irwin and, to a

lesser extent, Terry Phelan, were bloody terrible. And when it came to corner kicks the story was no better. The number of times Tommy Wright was able to take the ball unchallenged was downright embarrassing.

In the circumstances, I felt justified in having a go at them at half-time. I pointed out to them that we had created enough chances to be out of sight at that stage. But the way things stood, we were liable to be hit a sucker punch and lose the game. Little did I know!

To be fair, we lifted our performance in the second half, although neither Irwin nor Phelan were putting the crosses where they needed to be put, in the hope that somebody might get a touch on them at the edge of the six yard area. But they were better than in the opening 45 minutes, and again some good positions were opening up to us. But the finish, sadly, was no better.

Ray Houghton, with a free pot at goal, somehow managed to strike the goalkeeper's boot with the ball and then lofted one over the top, after big Niall had set it up for him. Eventually I take Ray off and he's clearly not impressed. He tells me that he's the only one making any chances and I answer, 'Yeah, but what have you done with them?'

In fact, the only one who has struck the ball properly in the match so far is Roy Keane, and that effort flew a foot or so outside the post, with Wright well beaten. Then Northern Ireland break. Ian Dowie, just on as a substitute, puts a ball in from the left; Kevin Wilson lays it back for Jimmy Quinn; and Quinn, with both feet off the ground, some 20 yards out, hits the sweetest of volleys over Packie's head into the net.

Bloody hell! We've dominated the game from start to finish and apart from one drive by

Wilson, which Alan Kernaghan blocked, and another from Michael Hughes, which was only just off target, they haven't threatened us. Now, they've just hit the jackpot and I go, 'Why the hell couldn't we have done something like that?'

The place erupts, and as the referee runs towards the centre spot to restart the game, somebody on the Northern Ireland bench – not Billy Bingham – gives us the two fingers and shouts, 'Up yours!'

Maurice Setters rightly complained but I tell him to forget it. We're a goal down and somehow we must get it back. Otherwise we're out of the World Cup for sure. I go for the first fall-back measure and bring in Alan McLoughlin.

Now Alan is not the strongest of players physically, and because of that I've never been convinced of his ability to work right across the line. But he's still a sweet accurate striker of the ball, and during his time with us he's shown himself to be capable of sorting out the final ball at the edge of the box.

His instructions are simple: he is to sit in behind the front two players and be ready to pounce on anything coming out of their penalty area. It's a wing and a prayer job but, bloody hell, it works; and just four minutes after Jimmy Quinn's strike, we're back in the game.

Irwin arcs a free kick from the right; a defender under pressure heads it out and McLoughlin takes it on his chest, looks up and with total composure puts the shot through the gap into the corner of the net. It's as neat and decisive as that. Suddenly, there's a smile on my face again.

A look at my watch tells me that there are just 13 minutes left in the game, and if it stays like this and there is a clear-cut result between Spain and Denmark, who are also playing tonight, we're

through. If both matches end in draws, we're gone.

I hear different stories about the way the game in Seville is going, but I can't be sure. To make certain of qualifying we must leave Belfast with two points and just before the end Niall Quinn has a chance of doing just that for us.

The cross from the right is inch perfect, but with time and space to take the ball on his chest and apply the textbook finish, he snatches at it and the ball goes wide. So much for those heart to heart talks in the Nuremore Hotel.

That should have been the icing on the cake for us. Instead, we are made to suffer bloody agony until the last shrill blast on the whistle tells us that the game is over.

Immediately Alan McLoughlin comes across to tell me Spain have won in Seville, and without waiting to ask him how he knew, I start hugging and congratulating the players on qualifying for the finals.

Then I catch Billy Bingham's eye. He tells me that he's happy we've qualified, and my response to that is something that will haunt me for the rest of my life. I go to complain to him about the guy who gave us the two fingers, but what comes out is something entirely different.

I point my finger into his eye and blurt, 'Up yours too.' The look on his face is one of astonishment, and as soon as the words are out of my mouth, I know that I've gaffed. I start to make a blundering apology, but Billy just turns and walks away from me.

Still hovering somewhere between fantasy and reality, I'm about to walk off the pitch when a fellow standing beside a television monitor shouts, 'Come and see the end of the Spanish game.' And the blood drains from my face.

I tell him the match is already over. He assures me it's not, and suddenly I'm suffering again. So what happens now if the Danes equalise and I have to walk into the dressing room and inform the players that it was all a ghastly error – that we're not going to the finals after all?

I walk away from the set, offer a few prayers into the night sky, and by the time I turn around again, the game in Barcelona is indeed over. Spain have beaten Denmark 1-0 and we've pipped the Danes for the second qualifying place in the group.

My joy is tinged with regret over the Bingham incident. And while the security people who looked after us so well during our stay in Belfast are anxious that we leave the stadium as quickly as possible to get to the airport for the return flight to Dublin, I am determined to make my peace with Billy before I leave.

With that in mind, I go to a room where he is holding his post-match press conference. And without waiting for him to finish, I blurt out my apologies in front of the assembled press men. Somebody told me later that I prefaced my interruption with the words, 'Don't worry Billy, I'm not going to flatten you' to which he replied, 'Forget about it Jack. You wouldn't be able to do it anyway.'

I'm not sure if that little altercation actually took place – it was all pretty hectic inside that room – but if it did, it was out of character with Billy's general attitude. He was big and magnanimous in wishing us well; and significantly, the Northern fans I met after the game were a lot more convivial than the people who had rained abuse on us all throughout the match.

Eventually, we took our leave of Windsor Park and, in truth, I've never been more relieved to see the back of a football stadium. By contrast, the mood of the crowd waiting to greet us on our arrival in Dublin could not have been more joyous. It was close to 1 a.m. by the time our plane touched down, but even at that hour there must have been between 2,000 and 3,000 fans waiting to welcome us home. There, too, was the Taoiseach, Albert Reynolds; and as the crowd sang and made merry, he was kind enough to tell us that we had lifted the entire country in qualifying for the finals. It's at moments like that that football can be most rewarding.

Outside the airport building the crowds were chanting that there would be no British in the finals, and in a peculiar way that saddened me. England's last chance of making it to America disappeared when Holland beat Poland earlier in the evening, and that left us as the only qualifiers from these parts.

Now we will be the team exposed to all the pressures of the publicity machine in 1994. Happy days ahead!

1 · December · 1993

I had just disembarked at Dublin, off a flight from Newcastle, when John Givens gave me the sad news. Niall Quinn had just undergone an operation on his knee at a hospital in Lancashire which meant that he wouldn't play again until after the World Cup finals in America.

Devastating! A day earlier, I read where Niall was to have a routine cartilage operation, and the expectation then was that he would be back playing within a month.

Now the news was infinitely bleaker. Apparently, when they opened his knee, they discovered that he had ruptured cruciate ligaments, and as any player will tell you, that is one of the most serious injuries in football.

I'm not sure whether I was sadder for Niall or myself when I first heard the news. More than most, perhaps, I realised just how much Niall had contributed, just how hard he had battled to get us to the finals. I had seen him give his all in places like Copenhagen and Seville, watched him battle against the odds in Belfast. Now, the whole thing was taken away from him.

It's in moments like that that you realise life can be very cruel. He would still be in America, of course, cheering us on from the side-line, but that's a far cry from being involved out there in the heat of the action. I recalled how he had gone to Italy for the 1990 finals as cover for Tony Cascarino, and had come back as a hero after taking over from Cass for the game against Holland in Palermo.

In the intervening period he had swapped clubs, leaving Arsenal for Manchester City ... and had become a better player for it. He was only one of four players who had taken part in all twelve of our qualifying games. Somehow it didn't seem right that we should have to go to the States without him.

My initial reaction, when informed of the situation, was that time was on our side, and who could tell what would happen over a period of seven months or so. But those slender hopes all but disappeared when the surgeon who performed the operation repeated that Niall would be out of the game until the 1994/95 season.

Slowly, inevitably, the bitter truth dawned that I needed a replacement for the finals. But where do I find him? At this long range it seems likely that Cascarino will take over Quinn's job in the finals, but that still leaves me short a player.

Our policy over the years was to keep one of our two front men in reserve, only making the substitution when we felt that a game needed a change of direction. Occasionally, we played Niall and Tony in tandem, but that was only in very exceptional circumstances.

Tony Cascarino has himself been in the wars with knee injuries, and my great fear is that he too might get into trouble and aggravate the situation. Unlike other, bigger nations we don't have the strength in depth to cope with setbacks like this.

Germany or Italy might be able to slot in a replacement in such circumstances without as much as blinking, but not so in our case. My immediate concern is to find another big player who can win the ball in the air, and in this context my thoughts are directed to Bradford.

There Frank Stapleton, a man who knows a thing or two about the job of fronting an attack, believes he has the solution for me in the person of Sean McCarthy. McCarthy had once represented Wales in a 'B' international game, but under new legislation introduced by FIFA, only those who have played in a competitive international game are deemed to have committed themselves to that country.

Maurice Setters has checked out McCarthy on a couple of occasions and is reserving judgment for the moment. Besides, word has just come through that McCarthy has been transferred to Oldham Athletic in a deal worth almost £600,000.

That is a good move for club and player. It is one thing to score regularly in one of the lower divisions; but if the lad has ambitions of making the grade on the biggest stage of all, it is imperative that he prove himself first at the highest level of club football. McCarthy hasn't yet done that, and I await his response to the Oldham challenge with some interest.

In fairness, his wasn't the only new name which has surfaced in the many discussions Maurice and I have had about the squad we would take to the finals. In the course of the qualifying series, it has become clear that some of the players who had given us such great service over the years are now coming to the end of the line.

At this point I'm not prepared to write off anybody. But I think that a couple of familiar faces might be missing when we take off for the States. It is time to go to Glasgow and take a look at Celtic's Paul Byrne.

We had Paul with us before on Under-21 trips, but judged on the reports I have been getting, his game has improved out of all recognition since going to Parkhead. When I saw the lad first he was overweight, but the word is that he has overcome this problem.

Lou Macari is playing him on the right side of midfield for Celtic. Eddie McGoldrick is the recognised stand-in for Ray Houghton in this position for Ireland. But if Byrne can do a job for me, I'm not about to send him away.

Another Celtic player recommended to me is Pat McGinlay, a left-sided midfielder who has scored a bundle of goals for his club during the first four months of the season in Scotland. McGinlay's big pluses are his flair for turning up in the penalty area at precisely the right time and, equally important, his capacity to operate down the left where we badly need additional cover.

Against that, however, I have doubts about his physical capacity to do the kind of job we demand of our midfield players. Scoring goals is a bonus, but the first requirement of the job is to run and graft for 90 minutes. And frankly, I'm not so sure if Pat is capable of delivering on that count. But the essence of a manager's job is perseverance. I'll go and check him out and if I feel he's the man for the job, you can take it from me I'll be up and down to Scotland in the New Year.

21 · December · 1993

The announcement that the draw for the World Cup finals would be held in Las Vegas on 19 December brought some familiar problems. Would I, for example, travel out to Las Vegas, or would I as I had done earlier, watch it on television in Dublin?

I was told that at least some of the other national team managers would be travelling to America; but after giving it some thought, I decided against joining them. There was, I felt, nothing to be gained by my being there, except as an information provider for people I had never previously met and would never meet again. And I didn't fancy the idea of hordes of people sticking microphones and tape recorders in my face. No, I would go to Dublin to a function sponsored by Opel in the American Embassy, where I would be surrounded by friends and where I could assess the implications of the draw without all the hassle of the 'live' show in Las Vegas.

The other problem about the draw was

Our last match prior to America was at Lansdowne Road where the fans gave us a great send-off (below). Unfortunately the Czechs caught us napping which didn't leave me feeling too good (right).

We're going to America.

understanding the bloody thing. For years people have been questioning whether the draw is 'rigged' or whether in fact it is truly open. Well, as a result of what I saw of the Las Vegas programme, I still don't know.

Sepp Blatter, FIFA's General Secretary, is a very suave man. But if the allegations about rigging are right, then he must be a magician for to the naked eye everything appears to be above board. And yet when the draw is finished, you are left wondering.

It's all a very complex business and it was complicated further by the manner in which it was structured in Vegas. The Republic of Ireland was classified as a second-seeded country in the draw, a decision based on our results in recent years.

Now the normal practice in World Cup draws is to start with your six top-seeded teams, then work your way down through the second, third, fourth flights, and so on. But this time it was different. For some reason or other they drew the second-seeded teams last and that made for a long, anxious wait for all of us.

In the end we finished up in the group headed by Italy and completed by Norway and Mexico. With two to qualify, it was immediately apparent that a lot of hard work would have to go into the mix if we were to get one of those two tickets and make it through to the second phase of the championship.

For months the speculation in the press was that we would be based in Boston if we qualified for the finals. In fact it went further than speculation, for even some members of the organising committee of US '94 appeared to support the idea. We, of course, had been in the Boston area in each of the preceding two years, and had attracted huge crowds to the Foxboro

Stadium. Given the Irish population of Boston that was hardly surprising, and it seemed to the world at large that basing the Irish team in the city made good commercial sense. From my point of view, the climate in Massachusetts at that time of year was ideal for football, and with thousands of our supporters in the stadium, we couldn't ask for a better home from home.

Imagine our disappointment, then, to discover that we had been put into Italy's group, and that the Italians, in turn, had been consigned to New Jersey. The Italians, like us, were hoping for Boston, but at least they would be conditioned for the heat and humidity of New York in June.

As luck would have it, the draw decreed that we should meet them in our first game in the Giants Stadium in New Jersey on 18 June. There couldn't be a much tougher opening assignment than that; but oddly, I was not too unhappy about it.

Experience teaches that the Italians tend to start slowly in competitions like this and then go from strength to strength with each consecutive game. If they are vulnerable, they are more likely to be found out early on, and to that extent I was reasonably satisfied.

The conditions in New Jersey would be different, but not as difficult I suspect as those in Orlando in Florida, where we play Mexico in our second game before returning to New Jersey to complete our programme against Norway.

To listen to some people talk, you would think that we never had warm weather back at home and that we were incapable of playing in the heat. That, of course, is plainly nonsensical; but having said that, it worries me that we shall have to endure conditions which even the Americans themselves find oppressive.

Moreover, I am just a little concerned that we

shall have to go in against Mexico in Orlando, which is not a million miles from home as far as they are concerned. I was in Mexico for the 1986 World Cup finals and one of the things I remember most was the sheer fanaticism of the locals anytime their team was in action.

The last thing I wanted for my players was to have to face that kind of partisanship in the stands. But I suspect that's what lies ahead. Given the relative distances involved and the numbers of Mexicans living in the United States, I can visualise a big Mexican presence in the stadium, and thousands more outside clamouring for tickets.

I'm told that the Republic of Ireland and Mexico have met only once – and that was in Eoin Hand's time as manager. The result of the game at Dalymount was a scoreless draw, but in view of the fact that it was played in 1985, it didn't seem to have much relevance now.

Mexico is a big footballing country, but in spite of the teeming millions in the country, they've never really got it together on days it mattered most. Occasionally they produce superstars like Hugo Sanchez, but never enough of them to lift the national team into the top bracket.

Yet, in the circumstances in which we'll meet them in Florida, they deserve respect. And I will underline that respect by travelling to see them play at the first available opportunity.

Ever since they beat England in Oslo, people have been going on about Norway and saying what a great team they are. But for me, that was one of the poorest English teams of recent years with a lot of changes, and it simply didn't gell on the night. England should have had them dead and buried at Wembley, but failed to put away their chances. In the end they paid for that when

the opposition got a late equaliser and a point they scarcely deserved. It has to be said that subsequently Norway went to Poland and came back with two points which clinched their place in the final. But the Poles were already out of contention at that stage and as such were not encouraged to play their strongest team.

This is the first time since 1938 that Norway has made it into the World Cup and I, for one, would not wish to diminish that achievement. In a sense, they've done a Republic of Ireland in their group and qualified on merit alone.

Beating England in Oslo was no big deal in my opinion. But some Irish people appear to think that it was. I could be wrong, but I don't share the view that they are one of the strongest teams going to the United States in the summer.

I'll be doing my homework on them in the coming months, but at this point I'm not too worried about them. I've seen many of their English-based players, and frankly they don't impress me as anything special.

What can I say of Italy that hasn't been said a thousand times before? Theirs is probably the best league championship in the world, and because many of the great international players from Europe and South America are involved, it tends to be always in the public eye.

I'm not particularly interested in the 'foreigners' playing in Italy. My interest is in those who will play in the Italian national team. And the first thing that needs to be said is that they have more high quality, technical players than possibly any other country in the world.

Despite what some commentators would have you believe, they are good competitors. Home or away they'll battle like Spartans, and the certainty is that if you get anything out of them you will have earned it.

It was Italy of course who ended our hopes in 1990, and reaffirmed a lesson I had been preaching to our players for years. You must never, ever allow teams to run through your midfield. If you do, you're dead.

On that unforgettable night in the Olympic Stadium, Kevin Sheedy tried to play a ball to the feet of John Aldridge when he should have put it down the line. That simple error cost us the game. With most of our players committed forward, the Italians simply poured through our midfield, and after three or four quick passes, Packie Bonner was picking the ball out of his net.

That was Italian football at its best. Once they control midfield, they'll push any number of people forward, but never before. Kevin Sheedy made the error and, boy, did we pay for it!

Among those who figured in the build-up to the goal was Roberto Baggio and it was no consolation to know that barring misfortune, Baggio would again be in their side in New Jersey. The good thing from our point of view was that since the Rome defeat, we had met Italy in Boston and proved that we were capable of handling their type of game. True, we lost 2-0, but both their goals came from set pieces, the first from a free kick, the other from a disputed penalty. Unless we are very careless or very unlucky, that is unlikely to happen again. Yet there is no escaping the fact that Italy in New Jersey represents a huge test at the start of our programme. To get the result we need, we will have to fight them, inch by bloody inch. And we will!

10 · February · 1994

For the past couple of days, my phone has been even busier than ever, and for once most of the queries have no direct relevance to football.

It's my health that's in the news, or more specifically a brain scan which I had a couple of days ago in the Mater Hospital. In all, it took perhaps no more than nine or ten minutes, but it's an experience I wouldn't want to repeat. It ended with the doctor telling me that he had good news. They had, indeed, located a brain, and yes, it seemed to be in reasonably good working order.

I first began to feel unwell during a holiday in Spain in January. It had been a hectic Christmas and before that, of course, there was the strain and the tension of those last two qualifying games.

I had watched more football than usual over the holiday period, travelling here and there to look at players before Pat and I and a couple of friends took off for Spain to unwind. The contrast couldn't have been greater, for from a situation in which I was living at a hundred miles an hour back home, I did absolutely nothing except eat and drink when I got to Spain.

Normally, of course, I go fishing for my relaxation, but that's out in January. And since I play very little golf these days, that left me with a lot of time on my hands and I just couldn't fill the time.

It came to a head one evening when I was discussing football – what else – with a friend and I tried to remember the name of a lad who once played on the left wing for Arsenal. I could see him in my mind's eye, as clearly as if he were in the room with me, but do you think I could remember his name!

Now, normally in that situation, you move on to another topic of conversation, but this time I couldn't. It was becoming an obsession. So I excused myself and left the house for a breath of fresh air. I walked for half an hour or so, when suddenly it came to me – Graham Rix.

That should have been the end of it. But it wasn't. When I eventually got to bed, I lay awake, inventing all kind of names and then trying unsuccessfully to bring them to mind. My head was on fire, and suddenly I found myself invaded by all kinds of self-doubt.

Unfortunately, things didn't get much better during the rest of the holiday and when I get back home I decided to see a doctor. I had been having trouble with my ears and part of the cleaning out process involved putting drops in them. That was only partially successful, however, and before I came over to Dublin I arranged with Martin Walsh, the team's medical officer, to have a complete check-up.

It included the usual things, like blood pressure and chest tests and, of course, that brain scan which I didn't fancy in the least. At the end of it, the official verdict was that I was stressed and needed to cut back on my programme considerably.

I have to admit that the stress bit was a surprise to me. Normally, I would consider myself to be a laid back person. True, there are times when I lose my cool in arguments about football, but that is the only subject which is likely to get my blood boiling.

From my youngest days, I could sleep on a clothes line. There could be pandemonium in a room, but if the notion took me, I'd be able to drop off within minutes. In fact, it is a lifesaver for me in situations in which I know that I'm going to be out until the early hours of the morning.

If I am required to drive, say 150 miles or more to an after-dinner speaking engagement, I will frequently get there a bit early, find a convenient place to park and then nod off for half an hour or so. Believe me, it's a tremendous help when the night begins to drag and people want you to linger.

Bearing that in mind, I was just a little upset to discover that medics had diagnosed stress. And yet, when I got to think about it, I ought to have seen the danger signs sooner.

Apart from the problem of qualifying, there were the spin-off problems which had to be addressed in a very short time. For example, I had advised the players against making any contractual arrangements until such time as we qualified, and having advised them on that point I was more or less obliged to fall into line. Then when we got that precious point in Belfast, everything had to be done in a hurry, and I think I was now paying the price of that policy decision.

Medical opinion was that I should cut back drastically on my non-football programme, but I explained that this was easier said than done. I came up through a school in which you didn't renege on commitments without a very good reason. And as I looked through my diary, I discovered that there was very little room for manoeuvre.

One of the things which could and did go was the meeting of World Cup managers in New York. Essentially, this was a talk shop, but in normal circumstances I would of course have gone. Out too was the meeting in Vienna to arrange the dates for the 1996 European championship qualifying games.

Instead, I took a week off down in Ballina, in which I just pottered about, doing little or nothing. It's the kind of place where you can relax. The local people are friendly and you can get on with life without too much hassle.

The other bonus was that my son John had returned home and was able to take care of the correspondence which was building up on my desk. Normally, I take care of that kind of thing myself, but now I just wanted to get out of the house and walk.

The worrying thing is that there is going to be little or no let up between this and the World Cup finals in June. If there's a downside attached to playing on the biggest stage of all in football, it is the thousand and one little chores which are thrust upon you and which have little direct bearing on preparing a team for the finals.

Take the media, for example. Day after day, I get calls from people wanting to set up interviews with me and I tell them that I just don't have the time to facilitate them. If they want a few words,

I'll deliver there and then. But appointments are out.

At this rate I'll be doing well to keep on an even keel until we get to the World Cup finals. But already I've made a few important long-term decisions. Once we get back from the United States, there will be no promotional or speaking engagements in September.

Back in the days when I was becoming disillusioned with club management, I tended to lose sight of the fact that there was a whole big world out there which had nothing to do with football. I rectified the problem then – and here I am in danger of making the same mistake all over again.

But this time, I hope to profit from those dearly bought lessons. As long as I'm involved with the Ireland team, I'll give the job one hundred and one per cent. But I'm equally determined, that on those occasions in which I find myself with free time, I'll enjoy them!

24 · March · 1994

I don't mind admitting that we made a bit of a gaffe over the first of the five warm-up games we had arranged for the World Cup finals – the one against Russia at Lansdowne Road yesterday.

This was an officially recognised international date, and we took it on the basis that it would help us to get clearances for most of the players needed for what would almost certainly be a fairly difficult game.

What we didn't realise, until it was too late, was that the Coca Cola Cup final was due to be played at Wembley just four days later. And with

no fewer than six of our players involved in the meeting of Manchester United and Aston Villa, that was, of course, disastrous from an Irish point of view.

England identified the problem much earlier than we did and had the good sense to bring forward their game against Denmark – the one in which Terry Venables took over for the first time from Graham Taylor – by a fortnight.

In our case, however, the problem was upon us before we really recognised it as such, and there was nothing for it except grin and bear the consequences. The question of cancelling the

The 2-0 win against Germany in Hanover really set us up for America. Andy Townsend celebrates the result with Phil Babb and Ronnie Whelan in the background.

Talking to the press after the Germany match.

fixture never really arose, for we needed a game in March after taking a conscious decision not to play in February.

It had been our practice for some time back to open our programme with a game in February, but gradually it became apparent that international games at that time of year were of no real value and were, in fact, something of an embarrassment when it came to securing the release of players. Clubs were very often involved in crucial cup or championship matches at that point and reacted accordingly.

Moreover, Lansdowne Road was unavailable to us until the last week in March, and if I had given the green light for a February date, it would of necessity have been played away from home. When you put the whole package together, it just wasn't worth it. And, of course, it upped the ante for the meeting with the Russians.

To be absolutely honest, there wasn't much I knew about the Russian team; but experience taught me that players from that part of the world are technically very strong and disciplined almost to a fault. Like ourselves, they were heading for the World Cup finals and as such would be looking for what people in the business call a 'result'.

It was against that background that I had to legislate for the loss of six players, including my entire first-choice midfield formation. Nor was that the end of it, for Terry Phelan pulled out with a hamstring, Alan Kernaghan had a recurrence of his groin trouble and, to cap it all, I discovered just a couple of days before the match that I would also have to make do without John Aldridge.

At that point I was worried, as you might expect. If you're lucky, you can get away with two or three changes in the side, but when you interfere with the basic structure of the team, you're heading into the realms of the unknown. And no manager can feel easy in that situation.

All the time, my mind was harking back to David O'Leary's testimonial game against Hungary in which we went two up after only ten minutes and still ended up losing 4-2. That was a match which we might have won 6-0, had I left well enough alone. But once you water down your team, anything can happen.

The difference now was that I could legislate before the game for certain contingencies. I balanced out the side as best I could, told them how they might avoid trouble and, more importantly, the things which could get them into difficulties if they weren't careful.

Necessity, they say, is the mother of invention, and with so many established players unavailable, I couldn't but be bold in my team selection. At right-back, for example, I had Gary Kelly, and that pleased me enormously for this is a full-back out of the ordinary!

A couple of weeks earlier he had been named as the best right-back in the Premiership and that surprised nobody. The problem, of course, is that Denis Irwin is already well established in our team at Number 2, and I don't have to tell you what a fine international player he is.

At centre-back, I went for Brendan Carey and Phil Babb – and held my breath. Brendan is a strong solid player who has been with us before. At times his concentration can waver, but I knew he could do a job for me in this game.

Babb was something else. People all over England were telling me what a very special player he is and how he could contribute to our World Cup plans. I went to watch him on three or four occasions and, to be honest, I couldn't make up my mind about him.

He was quick and he was mobile and those are priceless assets in any centre-back. He was also very composed on the ball, they said, and that worried me. I don't like composed centre-backs who are apt to put the ball at risk. Give me the guy who hoofs it over the stand rather than give it away to an opponent.

The other suspected weakness in his game was that he tended to be pulled all over the place by opponents. If the centre-forward, for instance, drifted out to the angle of the penalty area, Phil went with him and that again was foreign to our policy.

We don't expect our centre-backs to man mark. Their primary job is to compete and win the ball. I wondered aloud how Phil would adjust to that new challenge.

I first noticed Jason McAteer on television. Then I went to Roker Park one day to watch him play for Bolton against Sunderland, and he struck me as somebody out of the ordinary. I had no idea at the time that he qualified to play for Ireland, but with a name like McAteer I reckoned there was a fair chance that he was eligible to wear a green shirt.

Liam O'Brien was back in central midfield alongside Ronnie Whelan, and up front David Kelly had the chance to prove that he could handle the job Aldo normally did for us.

As I say, I was a bit apprehensive going into the game, but as it transpired I needn't have worried. Far from being turned over by the Russians, we gave them a bit of a pummelling and had we won by two or three goals, it would have been no more than we deserved.

Ronnie Whelan had three reasonable chances when clearances arrived at his feet just outside the penalty area. Now Ronnie is normally very good in those situations – remember that vital goal he scored against Northern Ireland at Lansdowne – but on this occasion he didn't even get the shots on target.

That was a disappointment, and it summed up our luck on a day when the ball never appeared to run for us in situations in which we had the Russians under the cosh. It was one of those days when from a very early stage we had to work hard and needed a lot of luck to put the ball in their net.

There was one occasion when Liam O'Brien teed up a free kick about 30 yards out and slightly to the left of the posts as he looked at them. He curled the ball almost perfectly, but while it cleared the end of the 'wall', it just caught the angle of the bar and upright and bounced 30 yards clear. Russia never created a chance of note, and as they trooped off the pitch at the end I thought they looked relieved.

So what were the good points? Well, the next morning one name leapt across the headlines. Gary Kelly of Leeds had caught the attention of the critics and almost without exception they singled him out as man of the match.

I too thought he had a great game. He looked easy on the ball, got down the line at every opportunity, and even the Russians were wide eyed about his acceleration over five or ten yards. If I didn't know beforehand that I had an embarrassment of talent at full-back, I certainly know now.

Gary, as I said, was brilliant but so too was young McAteer. For the first ten or fifteen minutes, he was undoubtedly the best player on the park, dominating his side of the pitch and putting in a few good-looking crosses.

Then the Russian manager paid him the supreme compliment. He withdrew one of his forwards, a small blond lad, and put him on

 Phil Babb was probably the find of 1994.

McAteer. Now when something like that happens, it means that the opposing manager has put his finger on the trouble spot and has taken the necessary corrective measure.

Naturally, Jason wasn't nearly as prominent after that and it possibly worried him. But I was at pains to reassure him that he had given the opposition most of their problems early on, and the fact that young Gary Kelly had hogged the headlines was in many respects down to him.

By withdrawing a player to mark Jason they left Gary free, and to his credit he made the most of it. But the roles might well have been so much different.

I was a lot happier about Phil Babb after the game than I was going into it. He did everything I asked of him, changed his game to suit our style and together with Brian Carey controlled the penalty area so effectively, that neither of our two 'keepers, Packie Bonner and Alan Kelly of Sheffield Utd, whom we used in the second half, got a lot to do.

Liam O'Brien in midfield looked a more rounded player than at any time in the past, and with Ronnie Whelan and Alan McLoughlin also doing their bit, we deserved more out of the game than the 0-0 result. Still, I'm not too dissatisfied.

28 · April · 1994

I felt like saying, 'here we go again', as I prepared the squad for the second of our World Cup warm-up games against Holland in the tiny Dutch town of Tilburg.

Given the circumstances, I thought we had done exceptionally well against Russia. The only disappointment was that the scoreline stayed blank at the finish, whereas we might have won by a couple of goals.

It was one thing taking on the Russians in your own back yard with a weakened team; the prospect of going to Holland without established players was a different matter.

There was no Paul McGrath or Alan Kernaghan in central defence. Denis Irwin and Roy Keane were out because of United's FA cup and championship programme, and on top of that, we had to make do without Tony Cascarino and John Aldridge.

At one point, it looked as if we would also be without Terry Phelan, and that gave rise to a curious situation. Phelan hadn't been in Manchester City's first team for weeks and my information was that he wouldn't be available to join us in Tilburg.

That left us very skinny for cover down the left. But with Steve Staunton available again for a place in midfield and Eddie McGoldrick capable of filling in at left-back, I knew we'd cope. Then I got the message that Arsenal had pulled McGoldrick out of the squad, and I saw red in more ways than one.

After all, Eddie hasn't been a regular first-team player of late for the club, and since this is a recognised international date I get back on to Arsenal like a flash. To give George Graham his due, he's very co-operative when I explain the position to him, and he immediately agrees to let us have the player.

Imagine my embarrassment then when Phelan walks into the team hotel the day before the game and tells me he is fit. Terry is too good a player to leave out, but having made a bit of a production to get Eddie to Dublin, I can't very well leave him on the bench, can I?

I would have to say that was the only position in which I was spoiled for choice. I looked at the players I had and decided that there were too many people in the wrong positions. Kevin Moran, out of favour with his club, would now be expected to fill the lead role in central defence and the midfield line looked misshapen.

McGoldrick, I decided, would go in ahead of Ray Houghton on the right; John Sheridan would join Andy Townsend in the central position; and behind them Ronnie Whelan would fill Paul McGrath's old role, sweeping in front of the back four. Up front, I named Tommy Coyne to take on the Dutch central defenders on his own, which had to be the toughest job of the day, by some way.

Privately, I shared the apprehension of many Irish fans who suspected that this was one of those rare occasions when we might get turned over and lose by two or three goals. I couldn't afford to transmit that message to the players, of course, and publicly I was making all my comments upbeat.

Having looked at the situation in some detail and pondered how to get the most from our limited resources, I decided I would tackle the Dutch the way I had seen the Danes tackle them. I instructed Packie Bonner to bounce his clearances off the Dutch central defenders, and I instructed the full-backs, Gary Kelly and Phelan, to push forward to pick up anything loose in midfield.

By deploying Ronnie Whelan in a sweeping role immediately in front of the two central defenders, Moran and Phil Babb, I expected him to be able to cover across for either of the two full-backs.

Coyne's instructions were simple. I wanted him to contest every high ball with the Dutch defence, I didn't expect him to win many of them, but I needed him to put the opposition under sufficient pressure in the jump for the ball that they wouldn't have time to direct the clearance accurately. With the extra players in midfield, we would then be expected to win the loose ball and build from there.

If everyone did their share of the work, I felt we might somehow escape – and we did. Coyne was simply magnificent, sparing nothing or nobody as he swept across the pitch like a radar beam, and prevented the central defenders directing their clearances with any kind of accuracy.

The Dutch like nothing better than to put five or six passes together in midfield, and once they succeed in making the tiniest opening, they'll run you. Well, they didn't run us in Tilburg, and in fact it wasn't until the start of the second quarter that they succeeded in putting more than two passes together – and even then, they didn't give us any problems.

After the first fifteen minutes or so, I turned to Maurice Setters on the line and said, 'Hey, I think we're in with a shout here', and he too sensed that something was on. By saturating midfield, we denied them the opportunity of getting at our back four. But even when they appeared to be getting to the pitch of the game, they caused us few problems.

In fact, Packie Bonner didn't have a shot of note to save in the first half, and it was much the same in the second half when we restricted them to a couple of hopeful long-range efforts. That was a tribute primarily to the way we held the centre of our defence, where Moran and Babb were equal to any demands placed on them by the Dutch.

Moran's ability to grow tall on the big occasion has long been acknowledged by those who watch Ireland play. Babb, of course, is a much more recent acquisition, but I thought he was bloody magnificent.

People had been telling me that he wasn't aggressive enough in the tackle. But he lacked nothing in aggression tonight. Others said that he couldn't tackle, but he tackled anybody who needed to be tackled and did it with the kind of pace and composure to impress even the cynics.

And what of young Gary Kelly at right-back? Like Babb, he had done well on his international debut against Russia, but now he was heading into the lions' den. The Dutch, intent on getting a win, had brought back all their foreign-based players and one of them, Bryan Roy, was pitted directly opposite Kelly, down the left flank.

Roy is one of the best left-sided players in the world and likes nothing better than to take the ball up to the full-back, throw a shape and then use his pace to get to the back line. The first time he tried it against Kelly, he lost the ball; the second time Gary outpaced him to prevent him getting in the cross. After that Bryan Roy simply never counted. If anybody had ever doubted Kelly's ability before, the youngster had now provided all the answers – conclusively.

Then, in midfield, there was the spectacle of John Sheridan in full spate. There were a lot of good players on the park at Tilburg, and it says much for Sheridan that he looked in a different class to any of them. Whether he was finding that extra yard of space for himself, changing the direction of the play with just one flick of the ball or sorting out the final pass through the middle, he was brilliant, and from a relatively

early stage I'm sure that Dick Advocaat, the Dutch manager, had identified him as the one they had to stop.

Try as they would, however, they couldn't put him out of the game and, fittingly, it was Sheridan who found the little touch of magic to provide the cross for the goal which won it for us early in the second half.

A precise, perfectly weighted pass from Ronnie Whelan carved the home defence in two and before they could regroup we were in. Ronnie picked out Sheridan with the pass and when he crossed from the right, Tommy Coyne and Steve Staunton were queuing up to put it in the net.

It was Tommy who was credited with the goal and nobody deserved it more. With an extra yard of pace, Coyne could be one of the best strikers in the world. He has a lot of skill on the ball, holds it long enough for the support to arrive, and even when the odds are stacked against him, he simply refuses to quit.

In the end, Tommy's goal was the only one of the game, although it has to be said that Holland went close to getting an equaliser in the closing minutes, when Ronald de Boer's header ran along the face of the crossbar before being booted to safety.

Had they scored in that instance, it would have been a rank injustice, for I thought we were the better team on the night and might have won it more easily with a bit of luck. Dick Advocaat admitted as much when we spoke briefly after the game and he was kind enough to say that Ireland had played very well.

Imagine my disappointment, then, when a journalist who interviewed me after the game sought to devalue our performance with the remark, 'Ah, but Holland didn't have Ruud

The victory
against
Holland in
Tilburg was a
great moment
in our warm-
up programe.
Here Eddie
McGoldrick
and the
Dutchman
Davids contest
the ball (top);
while Andy
Townsend
(below)
celebrates
victory.

Gary Kelly and Steve Staunton celebrate the first Irish goal in the famous 2-0 win over Germany in Hanover, one of the best results we've ever achieved. The Irish fans (below) certainly seem to agree.

Gullit or Marco Van Basten.' He made the remark apparently in all seriousness and I nearly hit the roof.

Bloody hell! Gullit and Van Basten haven't played for Holland for about two years, and here's this reporter advancing their absence as a reason for their defeat. What he didn't say was that Advocaat had called up his likely World Cup team at that point, including people like Ronald Koeman, Wim Jonk, Dennis Bergkamp and, of course, the de Boer twins, Frank and Ronald.

No, the Dutch were out to clobber us on their way to the States and that's what made it so special for me. They hadn't been beaten at home for ages and I sensed that football people all over Europe would look at the result in their papers the next morning and say, 'What's going on here?'

It was a lovely surprise and I know that the Irish public shared my sense of delight. It had taken us six months to get the stench of that terrible defeat by Spain out of our nostrils, but now at last we had succeeded. We could look the world in the eye again.

It has been a great occasion, not least for the fact that the 1,500 or so Irish supporters in the compact stadium roared us home as only they can.

When we eventually left the stadium, we discovered that a couple of inconsiderate Dutch people had double parked, and our coach was stuck there for the best part of an hour.

However, a couple of dozen pairs of strong Irish arms 'bounced' the offending cars out of the way and we made our way home. It's a night for celebrations.

12 · May · 1994

There have always been reservations in my mind about the merits of treating testimonial games as a means of preparing a squad for international fixtures. Such matches tend to fall into that limbo between light-hearted kickabouts and the real thing.

As such, I had serious doubts about the value of Kevin Moran's testimonial involving an Ireland XI and a team drawn from the FA Premiership as a reliable guide to our preparations for US '94.

To be honest, those doubts didn't disappear entirely after we had won 5-1. But I still judged it to be a worthwhile occasion.

For one thing, I was delighted to be associated with the tribute to Kevin. I read one of the pre-

match tributes which stated that no braver man ever played football – and I would agree wholeheartedly with that. He never hesitated to put his head where others were loath to risk their feet; but that was only half the story as far as Moran was concerned.

He was, and is, a very astute reader of the game and he belongs to a rare breed of players who are capable of lifting their game to fit the occasion. The bigger the game the better he plays, and if you need somebody to hold the fort when you travel abroad, you never have to look any further than Kevin.

Personalities apart, I reckoned the game could be useful to us in the sense that there were some very good players in the Premiership team. True, it was only a friendly game, but I thought it was a friendly game with a bit of an edge to it, and to that extent it had a part to play in preparing us for America.

For example, the Premiership attack was made up of Alan Shearer and Andy Cole, and I reckoned that if we could handle this pair with authority we could handle anybody. The sceptics said that we lacked pace in the centre of our defence. If we were, then Cole and Shearer, two of the most explosive runners in British football, would surely find us out.

In fact, nothing of the sort happened. Andy Cole has the kind of pace I often envy, the kind that enables him to get away from markers in even the tightest of situations. The commentary on the performance of our defence that night was that, with rare exceptions, neither Andy nor Alan really troubled us.

The other big point which came out of the game was that we can score goals when the mood takes us. As I said before, everything had to be measured against the fact that it was only a testimonial game. But as I viewed it, there was nobody getting out of the way and making the job of Tim Flowers any easier. And I would point to our third goal by David Kelly as a classic of its kind.

The ball moved first one way, then another, came back off a post, was pushed back into the area and eventually finished with superb skill. The crowd must have been on its feet for a full minute as the ball whizzed all over the place. Goals of that quality decorate any game.

People often point out to me – and they are absolutely right – that David Kelly has the highest strike rate of any Ireland player. And yet he always seems to be squeezed off the teamsheet for big games.

That, at the end of the day, has to be down to my judgment. I like centre-forwards who are not only sharp but physically strong enough to be difficult to knock off the ball. And for me, David just didn't have that kind of physical presence.

Now, at last, he appears to have put on some extra weight without sacrificing any of his sharpness in the 18 yard area – and I'm delighted. As a finisher, he's right up there with the best of them, and with the additional poundage, he is now a bigger headache than ever for opposing defenders.

The other point which encouraged me on the night was our first goal scored by John Sheridan. To the great majority of the crowd it was a freak score: John's shot from well outside the penalty area struck a defender before looping over Flowers. And yet that goal encouraged me, for it helped to emphasise a point which I had been trying to get across to the players for ages.

Time out of number, I had watched players like Keane and Townsend rampage through opposing defenders only to spoil it all by playing a pass too many. I kept preaching to them the value of attempting the occasional shot from outside the penalty area.

On the law of averages, you can expect to get at least one long-range shot on target and even if it deflects off another player, there is always the chance that you will get a favourable rebound. And yet you wouldn't believe how difficult it is to convince players to put their head down and 'have a go' from outside the 18 yard area.

I recall only too well, as many Irish fans will, that it was a freak goal by Lee Dixon, after the ball cannoned off Steve Staunton at Wembley, which gave England a very lucky 1-1 draw and eventually cost us a place in the finals of the

After the heroics against Holland and Germany, the home defeat by the Czech Republic in our last match before America was disappointing. Here Tony Cascarino (top) and Gary Kelly (below) tussle with the Czechs.

European championship.

Every soul in the 80,000 crowd that night knew that it was a Mickey Mouse goal, but they all count. And when I looked in the record books at the end of the year there was no mention of the word 'deflection'. All it said was that Dixon had scored and we were out of the championship.

Against that background then, John Sheridan's goal gave me particular satisfaction, and I hope that it will encourage others to have the occasional 'pot' at goal when we set down on American soil in June.

Above all else, however, this was Kevin Moran's night and the sight of 43,000 fans on their feet to salute him as he came on to the pitch with his children before the game will stay with me for a long time.

It was a great occasion for him, an encouraging evening for the rest of us, and I hope that out of it will come some good in the context of our World Cup programme.

26 · May · 1994

The furthest thing from my mind at the start of the year was that we would play Bolivia as part of our build-up to the finals. In fact, we had settled on Portugal as the opposition in our 24 May game in Dublin until the draw for the 1996 European championships put the two of us in the same group.

The Portuguese didn't fancy the idea of showing their hand in a friendly game before the real action started, and when a list of possible replacement countries was suggested to me, I chose Bolivia. In doing so, I was conscious of the need to vary our preparations as much as possible and to familiarise ourselves with any type of tactic we might encounter in the finals.

It was one thing sharpening our teeth against European-style teams, but what if we had to face a South American team in the States? It would be too late at that point to start revising our homework, so I decided that Bolivia, who were booked for a European tour in May, would do us nicely.

Apart from the fact that they had qualified for the finals for the first time through the orthodox system, I knew very little about the Bolivians. But of one thing I was certain. Like all teams from South America, their game would be based on pretty, tightly patterned moves, and it would present our players with a different kind of challenge

Against that background, then, I was glad to have all our established players back in the squad. Thankfully, the club season in England has now run its course and that means that Roy Keane and Denis Irwin are again available to us. Because of Manchester United's chase of the FA Cup, League Cup and championship treble, it has been an exceptionally tough season for everybody at Old Trafford and I'm anxious to see how our two players there have made out.

Also back in the fold is Paul McGrath, who has played only two games for Villa since the League Cup final at Wembley. It doesn't need repeating that Paul has had his share of injuries over the years, but his latest setback is different. He's been to see three specialists in the last two months or so, and it seems that nobody is sure whether his shoulder problem is down to a trapped nerve or the result of a viral infection.

I decided that we would go up to the Nuremore Hotel in Carrickmacross to prepare for a couple of days, as much to vary the routine as anything else. We had been to the hotel previously, of course, and with its many facilities, it proved an excellent place in which to prepare for a match.

The training itself was undertaken at Oriel Park in Dundalk, and it was there that I saw Paul McGrath work out for the first time since our game against Northern Ireland six months earlier. To be honest, I wasn't very impressed. He seemed to be out of condition. When he ran he gave the impression of 'carrying' his shoulder. There and then, I decided it would be best to leave him out of the Bolivian game and concentrate on sharpening him up in training.

Normally, we don't ask him to do too much in training, but in the belief that serious situations demand serious measures, I decided that this was neither the time nor the place for kid-glove treatment. He would have to work on his fitness and if he broke down in the process, so be it.

Unless things change drastically, the appropriate timetable for Paul will be for him to play the last 30 minutes of the game against Germany in Hanover next Sunday, and then the full 90 minutes in the meeting with the Czech Republic at Lansdowne a week later.

That will be our last competitive game before going in against the Italians, and there is no way that we can afford to go into that match with the fitness of a player like McGrath still unproven. Unfortunately, we will have to submit the names of our 22 World Cup players some forty-eight hours before the Czech games and to that extent, we will have to 'go blind' with Paul.

But the man has been so influential in the development of the team, so reassuring to those around him when he is playing well, that it is a risk which we simply must take.

Meanwhile, I decide to go with a partnership of Phil Babb and Kevin Moran in central defence against Bolivia, and that will revive memories of our brilliant backs-to-the-wall stand in Holland.

I named Packie Bonner for his 72nd international appearance to equal the record which Liam Brady established a couple of years ago. Mindful of what happened in Tilburg, I went with an extra midfielder in place of a second specialist forward alongside Tommy Coyne.

Against the Dutch I asked Ronnie Whelan to sit in front of the back four and he did the job superbly. In line with the need to experiment, I now gave the position to John Sheridan on this occasion and paired Roy Keane with Andy Townsend in the central positions.

The opening 20 minutes or so went much as I expected. The Bolivians knocked the ball about among themselves, but they showed no inclination at all to come and play us. The instruction to our players was to sit back and watch how the game developed and then go and attack them.

The great danger in those situations is that people go diving into the tackle and when they miss, they put everybody else in trouble. Even when the South Americans were in possession 60 or 70 yards from our goal, the two front runners were still making off-the-ball runs, all good experience for our defenders.

We created one or two chances in the

 Sweating it out in Orlando: Kevin Moran and Mick Byrne.

Gimme water! Alan Kernaghan in Orlando.

opening half. One in particular might have brought a goal. Andy Townsend knocked down a cross from Steve Staunton, but instead of taking the ball early, Tommy Coyne waited and eventually found himself without an angle.

As the teams went off at half-time, there was some good applause, which was encouraging. The reaction of the crowd can sometimes give you a message you don't want to hear. But the converse of that is that it can lift a team when it's most needed. Now they appeared to be happy with what they had just seen, and that pleased me.

Nevertheless, I still had some forceful things to say when we closed the dressing-room door at half-time. I reckoned that we could do better and I told the lads that it was time to go and chase the game.

I also decided to make some changes, not that I was dissatisfied with the overall performance, but I felt I should look at players like Alan Kernaghan and Jason McAteer in the second half. Alan's performance would be of particular interest to me for, like Paul McGrath, he'd had a rough time through injuries. At his best, he had a lot to contribute to the team and I wanted to see how a protracted absence had affected his game.

As it transpired, I thought we played a lot better after the interval. During our half-time talk, I pointed out to Roy Keane and John Sheridan the advisability of swapping roles, and it worked to perfection. Whereas John had stayed and 'minded the shop' in the first half, he now had a licence to get forward and put extra pressure on the South Americans.

It all added up to a situation in which we began to get in behind the defence, and there were a couple of occasions when the Bolivians survived in situations in which they had no right

to expect a reprieve. One which comes immediately to mind was a cross from the right by Roy Keane, which somehow managed to elude the Irish and Bolivians alike until it arrived with Steve Staunton at the far post. Steve is usually deadly in those kinds of situations, but in this instance he drove the ball into the side netting.

That was one of the few things he did wrong for the whole evening; but in spite of the pressure, nothing was happening in terms of goals. Then I sent on Tony Cascarino in place of Tommy Coyne who had run his legs off, and as so often happens it coincided with the goal which won the game for us in the closing minutes.

Cass knocked one down for Terry Phelan and when his shot struck a defender, the rebound, luckily for us, ran directly to John Sheridan 25 yards out. When John catches the ball properly, he can be deadly from that kind of range. Right from the moment the ball left his foot, he knew he was on a winner and the Bolivian goalkeeper never moved a muscle until the ball had hit the net. It was a goal to win any game, and with so little time left there was simply no way back for the Bolivians.

I don't think the South Americans could in honesty complain about the 1-0 scoreline. But with my hand on my heart, I have to admit that we could have gone one down before Sheridan scored. In an isolated attack, Julio Baldiesco, who had impressed me as the best of the Bolivians, beat a tackle on the edge of the penalty area and with the outside of his boot tried his luck with the shot. It caught Packie going the wrong way, but fortunately for us it also caught a post and bounced to safety.

That was a stroke of luck, but had it gone in I would have felt hard done by. Over the course of the 90 minutes we were far and away the better side, and had proved conclusively that we were capable of dealing with the South American type of game.

On the debit side, I have to say that my pre-match fears about Keane and Irwin were substantiated. Keane looked anything but sharp, and Denis was perhaps even more sluggish before I replaced him with Gary Kelly.

Given the season that they've been through with Manchester United and the pressures that go with playing in a successful United team, I suspected that both our lads would feel the pinch by the end of May.

I only hope that a change of surroundings and a licence to take things easy in training will do the trick, and get them buzzing again before we set foot in America!

27 · May · 1994

I wasn't greatly bothered when I first got the phone call telling me that I was to be made a Freeman of Dublin. I don't mean to sound blasé or opinionated in saying that, but ever since I was a lad at Leeds United, I had been in the public eye to some extent and you get accustomed to calls asking you to attend this or that function.

So when I got the word some time in February that the Lord Mayor of Dublin was to confer some honour or other on me, I wasn't exactly doing handstands. After all, I'd once been made an honorary Irishman by Charlie Haughey and that didn't create too much interest among the public.

It was only when I got to the presentation area in College Green in Dublin that I knew I was guilty of a monumental miscalculation. This was no routine award ceremony – and there were thousands of Dubliners out there on the streets to prove it.

Only then did the dimensions of the honour which was about to be conferred on me come into focus. Only then did I feel privileged and suitably fortunate to be the recipient of the city's highest award.

Up there on the stage were all the civic dignitaries, including the Lord Mayor, Tomas MacGiolla. There, too, were some of my best Irish friends including Des and Mary Casey, and others who had travelled to Dublin for the occasion. All the members of the squad were present, of course, and I was delighted to see old international players like Con Martin, Tommy Eglington and Arthur Fitzsimons also on the podium.

The Lord Mayor, in his address, referred to me as a special Englishman and, to be honest, I felt a bit special just then. What appealed to me most was the fact that I was the first Englishman to receive the honour this century. The last one apparently was a plumbing contractor who undertook a major scheme in the city in the mid-1850s.

Somebody told me that as a freeman I was now entitled to herd my sheep over the bridges leading into the city and that I could use the urban refuse tips without charge. The Lord Mayor disillusioned me on both counts, but reassured me that I would get to write my signature in a very distinguished book. When I eventually signed, I knew exactly what he meant.

Yabadabadoo! Roy Keane and Andy Townsend at Universal Studios.

The Irish team that beat Italy 1-0 in the Giants Stadium.

Paul McGrath gave one of the greatest displays of his life against Italy.

The signature immediately above mine belonged to no less a person than Mother Theresa of Calcutta. And further back great people of the stature of John F. Kennedy, Nelson Mandela and the Pope had entered their names in the book. It was a tremendous honour for me to be allowed to join them in receiving the freedom of Dublin, particularly since only sixty-two people in history have been so honoured.

Talking to the crowd afterwards, I reminded them that my real name was John Charlton. The only person who ever called me correctly was my schoolmaster up in Ashington. He used say to me, 'Bend over John.' I think a lot of people listening to me identified with that situation.

On a more serious note, I paid tribute to the members of the squad, and deservedly so. I was stepping up and accepting the kudos, but essentially it was a collective award, a tribute to the players and backroom staff who had worked so hard to get us where we are.

I thanked them in particular for their willingness to listen. You may talk all you like to people, tell them right from wrong, but if they're not ready to hear the message, you're wasting your time.

The mark of this Ireland squad is their readiness to listen. And having taken the advice on board, they then go out and try to put it into practice. That kind of attitude is coveted by every manager and I count myself lucky to be able to work with players like that.

I'm sure that the people back in Ashington would have been chuffed to discover that one of their own had made it to the top in Dublin, and that a miner's son had joined some of the most famous people of the century on the city's roll of honour.

For me, it was the high point of a love affair with Ireland and the Irish. I've now been involved with the Irish team and the Irish people since 1986, and I can honestly say that they've been eight of the happiest years of my life.

My association with Ireland goes back a long way to my early days at Leeds United, and one of my first trips across the Irish Sea took me to Waterford for a game at Kilcohan Park. We flew to Cork and then completed the remainder of the journey by road.

There wasn't too much money around in those days, and instead of the luxury coach which would be available for visiting teams in the modern game, we set off for Waterford in a convoy of cars. Fortunately or otherwise, the driver of our car was more interested in the pubs than the beauty spots along the way.

Every pub we came to had either the best pint, the best half one, the best ale and so on – and, of course, we had to sample the product. It was one of the most hilarious journeys I've made in football, and by the time we made it to Waterford, Billy Bremner and I were well sozzled. We enjoyed it immensely, but I don't think Don Revie was very pleased.

Since taking the Ireland job, my travels have brought me to every nook and cranny in the country, and I've grown to love the place even more. At the end of the day, I think it is down primarily to the friendliness of the people.

There is among certain people in Britain a reservation about coming across to visit Ireland. And when you look at some of the horrific pictures coming out of Ireland, either on television or in the written press, that is not greatly surprising.

Any time I speak at a public function in England, I try to correct that impression and assure people that English visitors to Ireland are at no greater or lesser risk than anybody else in the country. Indeed, except for the terrible Mountbatten murders, no English visitor to the country has come to harm since the start of the present troubles.

That is a message I seek to get across at every opportunity. The positive side of the marketing operation should deal with the unique facilities which Ireland can offer its visitors.

As a man who enjoys fishing, I can vouch for the fact that the West of Ireland, in particular, is a fisherman's paradise. And in a wider context, the chat and the fun in Dublin is like nothing to be found anywhere else.

These are just two of the selling points for the country and, of course, there are many, many others. Ireland has a lot going for it, but we live in a very commercialised world and everything demands the hard sell.

It may be only football, but I like to think that our team has played its part in that process and helped, even in a small way, to put Ireland in the frame.

30 · May · 1994

Ever since I became involved in international football as a player in Alf Ramsey's England team, I was aware of the significance of games involving German teams. Just as Brazil identified all the characteristics of South American football, Germany was the team by which all others measured their standards in Europe.

Like the Italians, they operate from a base of a strong national championship, a huge advantage for any national team manager. At any given time the Germans could put two or three national squads in the field, any one of them good enough to do the business.

As such, I was a little apprehensive when I agreed that we should play them on German soil at a stage when their preparations for the defence of the World Cup would be pretty well advanced. On the other hand, it would be a perfect opportunity to assess our progress. But against that, there was the nagging doubt that we might get a hiding.

Now, the game was virtually upon us and whatever self-doubt there may have been, it was time to get attitudes right and ensure that when we got to Hanover we'd be as competitive as ever.

The day after the Bolivian game we went to London for a charity dinner, and I was happy that it gave us an opportunity of meeting some of our supporters on the other side of the Irish Sea. These people have been fantastic, travelling with us all over Europe, and I value their patronage.

It goes almost without saying that they are mostly Irish emigrants or the offspring of Irish emigrants, but not exclusively so. You'd be amazed the number of ordinary English, Scottish and Welsh who have aligned themselves with us for no other reason than that they like the type of game we play.

We travelled to Hanover on the day before the game, and that brought back memories of the day in 1988 when we played on this same ground against the Soviet Union in the European

Andy
Townsend
outpaces
Tassotti.

Ray Houghton goes head over heels after scoring the winner against Italy; while the Irish fans (below) celebrate.

championships. That, to my mind, was one of our best ever performances and it brought back pleasant memories of that spectacular volleyed goal by Ronnie Whelan.

It was good to have Ronnie with us again, but I wasn't quite sure if I would play him on this occasion. My original intention was to continue the process of experimentation, but then somebody handed me the German teamsheet and I began to think again. In my opinion this was Berti Vogts's strongest team, and whatever about me he certainly wasn't in the mood to take undue risks.

I went and talked it over again with Maurice Setters, but I eventually decided that I'd stay largely with my original thinking. The sports writers with us were full of the fact that Packie Bonner would break the record for Republic of Ireland appearances in this game. But I had other ideas.

Alan Kelly was knocking on the door for recognition and while he had come in for a couple of games with us, I considered that he hadn't been fully tested. This was the occasion which would fill that void – if he could stand his ground under German fire, he could handle anything in international competition.

I was determined also that this would be the day for young Jason McAteer to earn his keep. Like Alan, he had shown a lot of promise in his earlier Ireland games, but now he would have to up his game still more.

Originally I had intended to start Gary Kelly at right-back, in view of the fact that Denis Irwin had taken a knock in the Bolivian match. But while I'd paired Kelly and McAteer on the same flank against Russia, I wasn't particularly keen on starting with two inexperienced players now. So I asked Denis how he felt about playing and

when he jumped at the chance, I said I'd put him in for the start and then probably bring on Gary for the second half.

All that was straightforward enough. But the problem which kept flooding my mind concerned Paul McGrath. The original plan was to give Paul 30 minutes in the German game and a full match against the Czech Republic. But since I was required to submit the names of my 22 players for the finals before that fixture, I decided that I had to know sooner or later how Paul was fixed. So I put him in the starting line-up and held my breath.

We went to the ground for our training session a bit earlier than scheduled, just to have a look at the Germans who were out before us – and it did my confidence no good at all. They looked so big and powerful, almost intimidating, and I remember turning to Maurice and saying, 'Anything we get out of this game, we'll have to earn.'

Significantly, the German players stayed on to watch us train. Perhaps they may have been thinking the same thing. It was at times like this that you felt reassured by that win over the Dutch.

Any notion that this was a mere knockabout for the Germans was dispelled when we got to the stadium on match day. There were 54,000 spectators inside and, it seemed, as many more outside it, all straining for the chance to see their team on its last appearance before leaving for America.

The certainty that Berti Vogts meant business was reinforced in the opening ten minutes, when they hit us with virtually everything they had. But our defence stayed cool, and a good save early on by Alan Kelly had the effect of giving extra confidence to those in front of him.

For our part, we tested out their defence with a couple of promising attacks, and after the game settled I think they realised they were in for a difficult day – a lot more difficult than they possibly imagined.

I was intrigued by the German tactics of playing a sweeper, Matthäus, behind two centre-backs, Kohler and Buchwald, even though we had only Tony Cascarino up front. That struck me as a waste of manpower; but then again Vogts may have realised that in Roy Keane and Andy Townsend we have two of the best midfield runners in Europe. And when you're accustomed to playing with a sweeper, as the Germans are, the risk of being caught flat by either Keane or Townsend in an orthodox back four formation was one which Berti was not keen to take on board.

On those occasions when Matthäus got forward into midfield, he caused us a bit of bother. But I had warned our players in advance of the danger of allowing him to measure the final pass. When players like Klinsmann and Riedle are allowed to turn and the ball is played alongside them, they are deadly.

But if you pressurise the player making the last pass, you eliminate the threat at source and that is precisely the game we inflicted on the Germans in Hanover.

Eventually Vogts replaced one of his central defenders, Buchwald, and brought on a midfielder, Berthold, but not before Big Cass had sown the seeds of a German disaster with the opening goal midway through the first half. It scarcely came out of the blue for we had already opened up the home defence on a couple of occasions before the score arrived.

McAteer did extremely well to get to the back line and when he measured the cross to the inch, the Germans may have sensed that they were about to go a goal down. Strunz, under pressure from Staunton, could only knock the ball back across the six yard area and Cass's firm header did the rest.

One of the things which struck us on our arrival at the ground was the humour of the crowd. It was like Mardi Gras time as home supporters mixed with the Irish, and the place fairly rocked with song and humour.

But I sensed that the mood changed as the game got even more competitive after the interval, and as the home team sought in vain to find a way back, the crowd got after them. We brought in Gary Kelly and Ronnie Whelan at half-time and they complemented a defence which had looked rock steady in the opening 45 minutes.

There were a couple of close shaves in our penalty area. But the reverse was also true, and 20 minutes or so before the end, Gary Kelly got the insurance goal with a shot which deflected off Martin Waguer on the way to the net.

In fact, we ought to have had a third goal. Andy Townsend was so surprised to find himself in the clear in front of goal that he hesitated, fatally, and was dispossessed in a situation in which he should have put the ball away without any bother.

Then it was over, and as I started back towards the dressing rooms, Maurice chuckled, 'Hey, we've just beaten the world champions on their territory. This is going to make some reading around Europe tomorrow morning.'

As a rule, I don't get too excited about friendly games, but it's difficult to get a result like this against a team like Germany and not feel elated. We've gone and achieved a result to better even the one we had in Holland – and we've done it purely on merit.

Water for Steve Staunton and Tommy Coyne in the Italy game. Water was the most controversial talking point of the first week of the finals.

Townsend and Massaro.

Tommy Coyne ran and chased to the point of exhaustion in the great win against Italy. Here he jumps against Franco Baresi.

I'm particularly happy with the contributions of some of the newer lads. Jason McAteer was great, Gary Kelly had a fine second half and apart from one second-half mistake, Alan Kelly in goal was brilliant.

Alan stayed on his line when the ball was played through the middle and in that instant almost cost us the game. Those are errors you make only once. Otherwise, the lad was quite superb.

The youngsters were great, but if there was one aspect of the game which pleased me more than anything else it was the return to form of Paul McGrath. There was one unnerving moment early on when he fell heavily and everybody looked instinctively at his suspect shoulder.

Fortunately, Paul was able to pick himself off the ground untroubled, and went on to play with all his old authority in the air. After all the anxiety of the last few weeks, I now feel more confident about his World Cup prospects.

1 · June · 1994

If there were prizes on offer for the person or persons who correctly forecast the names of the 22 players I would take to the World Cup finals, I reckon they might have had to split it a couple of thousand ways.

The fact is that once certain players had established their fitness, the squad virtually picked itself. With the evidence of the German game to guide me, I needed not much longer than the time it takes to write down 22 names.

That is not to imply that I didn't cast the net as wide as I could. I did. But as the months went by and the build-up programme to the finals progressed, I was pretty certain about the people I wanted with me.

Packie Bonner had a difficult season at club level but it didn't really alter my opinion of him. He's always done the job for Ireland, and if you go back over the years, he's made precious few mistakes at international level.

In fact, I think he was harshly treated by Celtic in their decision to let him go at the end of the season. But new managers like to put their stamp on things and it was just Packie's misfortune that he was one of the players singled out by Lou Macari for the long walk.

Alan Kelly first came to my attention seven years ago as a goalkeeper who had a future in international football. But then, with everything going for him, he went and broke a leg twice in successive years. In a sense, that's been the story of his life even this season. At a time when he was making his play for a place in the Ireland squad, he had to fight off a challenge from Simon Treacy to establish himself as the Number 1 at Sheffield United.

In my book, however, he is among the best 'keepers in Britain and I liked the way he handled the pressure when he got his chance in Germany. With two 'keepers like these, I'm not going to worry too much when we get to the States.

Denis Irwin is regarded by Alex Ferguson as the Mr Consistency of Manchester United and it's not hard to see why. He very rarely has a bad game, and when the chips are down he's a good lad to have with you. More than that, his ability to strike the ball well is a big plus in set-piece situations.

I don't think we saw the best of Denis in our build-up programme and that almost certainly was down to the tough season he had at Old Trafford. But I'm hoping that a short rest and a new environment will do the trick for him in America.

Gary Kelly is one of the young men who have brought a new sense of excitement to the Irish camp. When his fellow professionals set out to name the best team in the Premiership this season, they named Gary for the right-back position – and there is no higher compliment to be had in the game than that.

His strengths are his phenomenal pace and his willingness to use it getting down the line. Additionally, he's no mean performer when it comes to long throw-ins. Here is one of those emerging players who, with luck, can be around for a very long time.

Terry Phelan, like Packie Bonner, has had a bit of an up-and-down season with his club, but I certainly have no complaint to make about the quality of his international performances. There are those who would say that he is not aggressive enough in the tackle, but this is only because he has so much pace in recovery, that it doesn't worry him too much if he fails to close down an opponent.

With his kind of pace, he's a good defender against one-two moves, and in a situation in which some of our central defenders are not the quickest, I value his presence in the squad.

Eddie McGoldrick is the kind of utility man whom every manager wants on occasions like this. He'll do any one of three or four jobs for you and he's particularly valuable to us in the sense

that he can cover down either flank.

Going to Arsenal has not been the great move it once looked for him but on those occasions when we drafted him, for international football, he did the business quietly and efficiently. He will be particularly useful if we happen to hit injury problems during the finals.

Paul McGrath has been the player who caused me most worry over these last few months. I first heard of his shoulder problems early in March, and ever since I've scarcely stopped thinking about them. Given that he played only two games for Aston Villa since their League Cup win over Manchester United in the last week of March, that's not surprising.

At his best Paul is a world-class player, but in spite of his super show in Germany I still worry. Although not as quick or as mobile as he once was, he's a first-class reader of the game, and with his kind of experience not too many people get past him.

Kevin Moran is the man who perhaps best identifies the competitive spirit in the team. He'll give you 100 per cent every time he pulls on a shirt, and in modern football that's a huge recommendation for any player.

At one point I had more or less resigned myself to the fact that he was finished at the top level. But he simply refused to allow me to write him off and, judged by some of his performances in the qualifying games, he will not let the side down if we press him into service again over the next few weeks.

Alan Kernaghan has not, as yet, produced his best form for Ireland, but I'm convinced that over the next six or eight years he is destined to become one of the men around whom future managers will build their teams. He'll never win prizes for pace, but in almost every other respect

Donadoni is closed down by Terry Phelan towards the end of the Italian game.

It's over! We've beaten the Italians and this is how we reacted on the bench.

After the great win against Italy, the defeat by Mexico was a huge disappointment. Time after time, we were foiled by the colourful Campos, seen here beating Tommy Coyne to the ball.

his game is sound. He's strong and competitive in the air and, most of all, he is aggressive in the tackle. I like that quality in any centre-back and it reinforces my belief that, in time, he'll emerge as a splendid international player.

Phil Babb didn't impress me at all when I first went to watch him on the recommendation of friends. But I have to admit that in the last three months he has proved my judgment wrong and gone from strength to strength with every game. He still does the occasional thing which irritates – like taking too much out of the ball in situations which call for first-time clearances – but he's quick and athletic, and in spite of his relative immaturity I believe he has a big job of work to do for us now.

Ray Houghton has been with us from day one and while he would be the first to acknowledge that his season at Villa was a bit 'iffy', he has the experience and competitive instincts to do the business for us if we feel that these are the qualities which are needed on the day.

If I had a complaint about Ray in the earlier games in the competition, it was that he tended to turn up in places where he had no right to be, and this occasionally stretched us when the ball was lost. But he would argue that it was his tireless running off the ball which gave us that little extra when it was most needed.

Jason McAteer, I don't mind saying, didn't figure in our plans at the start of the season. Then I went to watch a match up in Sunderland and, as was the case when I first saw Houghton back in 1986, he struck me immediately as a lad who could do a real job for us.

He's young and he's capable of lasting any pace. At this point he doesn't have the background of the other players in the squad, but I thought he came of age as a player in that game

in Hanover. It was there that I decided he would be in the squad for America.

Roy Keane is rightly acclaimed as one of the best young players in Europe and in searching out the reasons for Manchester United's remarkable season, you would have to say that it was his partnership with Paul Ince which more than anything else kept the team motoring on difficult days.

The thing that sets him apart from others of his age is his phenomenal engine. He'll go for the full 90 minutes, and while he too is showing signs of the price United had to pay for their cup and championship double, he can be a big fish in a big pool in the finals.

Andy Townsend's name was the first name down on paper, not just because he skippers the team but he is, in a very real sense, the fulcrum of the team. Like Roy, he can be devastating going forward, but the mark of his professionalism is that when required to stay put and anchor midfield, he is disciplined enough to do it.

Andy had fitness problems at Villa at the start of the season which were largely responsible for the fact that he took time to settle into Ron Atkinson's team. But his contribution in all twelve qualifying games was substantial and I'm confident that he can keep it going in the States.

John Sheridan may occasionally have felt that he was never going to establish himself in the team but all that changed on the day we beat Holland in Tilburg and I realised there was no way that he could continue to be kept out – even if it meant going with an extra midfielder.

As a distributor of the ball, he's always been in a class of his own, but back in the early days, he wasn't too keen on tracking opponents. He is now prepared to do this and he is a much better player for it.

Alan McLoughlin is one of those players who, when I leave him out, will invariably come on to me and ask what he's done to deserve it. And the truth is that more often than not he's right. He is another fine striker of the ball and if you watch him closely, you'll find that he times the run better than most when moving on to the return pass.

I have never regarded him as strong enough physically to do the 90-minute running job that we demand of our midfield players. But as he showed against England in Sardinia and again in the Northern Ireland match in Belfast, he's a great player to have on the bench if a game needs a change of direction.

Stephen Staunton has probably been our most effective player of the season, and the great thing is that he's getting better all the time. He's strong and he's aggressive, and now that he has acquired the confidence to take on full-backs and get to the back line, he is a real matchwinner.

He started out of course as a full-back, but as was the case with Paul McGrath and Mark Lawrenson, I reckoned that he had too much ability on the ball to be left there. Together with Denis Irwin, he gives us valuable options in dead ball situations.

Ronnie Whelan, had he stayed fit, would have been the man to anchor the team these last four years, but unfortunately his career was dogged by one injury after another. Indeed, many a lesser player would have caved in completely in the kind of situation in which he found himself, and it is a tribute to his character that he's got himself back to the top level.

He lost four of the best years of his fine career through fitness problems, but his display against Holland and again when I brought him on for the second half of the German game proved that

he has the know-how and the discipline to anchor midfield if asked.

John Aldridge, like all great strikers, does his best work in the six yard area. But in our game plan he is also required to range across the width of the pitch putting defenders under pressure when they have the ball. To some this may imply something of a contradiction, but Aldo is the living proof that it works.

John's pushing on a bit now and no longer has the kind of pace which gets him away from opponents. But with his proven temperament and guile, he'll not be found wanting when the call comes.

Tommy Coyne has put together one of the great recoveries in international football this season, for it has to be remembered that he wasn't even involved at club level when we resumed our qualifying programme in September.

I've always said that with an extra yard of pace Tommy could be of the best strikers in the world – and I still hold to that view. He's a good header of the ball, can hold it up well until the support arrives, and has the intuitive skill to know exactly where the net is. More than that, he's a very brave lad.

Tony Cascarino is another skilful target man. He is not as effective on the ground as Tommy Coyne, but his strength and tenacity in the air more than makes up for it.

There is a similarity between Alan McLoughlin and Cass in the sense that in the past, I've tended to use him as a replacement. But faced with a situation in which I had to improvise in the absence of Niall Quinn, I turned to Cass, and he was equal to the challenge.

I've always regarded David Kelly as a very good mover who can take up excellent positions left or right. But he's unlucky in the sense that

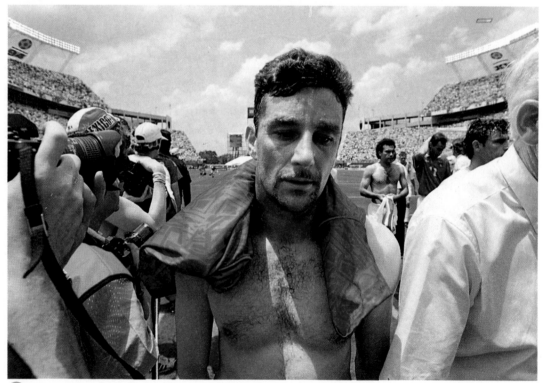

One Irish fan (top) made the best of it against Mexico, but you can see the disappointment in Aldo's face (below) at the end of the match. Still it was his late goal that got us out of the Group of Death.

For the Norway match I was kicked upstairs, so I watched the game from the stands with Sean Connolly and my son John (top). John Sheridan beats Bjornebye (below).

he's fallen between two stools: not strong enough to do the kind of job Tommy Coyne performs, or tenacious enough to hit the same work rate as Aldo.

But he's put on some weight this season and I think his game is the better for it. That goal he struck in Kevin Moran's testimonial game was as good as any I've seen recently and he's in the squad on merit alone.

Those then are the players in whom the country has reposed its trust and I don't think they'll be found wanting. Of course there were hard luck stories such as that of David O'Leary. Had David played a full season with Leeds, it is possible that he would have been coming with us. But because of his injury troubles, that unfortunately wasn't a starter.

Liam O'Brien was another name on my mind, but the biggest heart-break of all was having to go without Niall Quinn. More than most, he had done his bit to get us to the finals. Now that we're there, we'll spare nothing or nobody in the task of ensuring that all the good work will not go unrewarded.

5 · June · 1994

There was an unmistakable feeling of fulfilment on the flight back from Hanover. We had just gone and beaten the world champions on their own patch, and the players who had toiled so hard to make it possible were entitled to walk with an extra spring in their step.

As the manager of the team, I too shared their sense of elation. It was good that they should experience the satisfaction which comes with beating the best. But there is sometimes a thin dividing line between confidence and complacency, and it was my job to ensure that they didn't stumble over it.

In my heart of hearts I was less worried about the feelings of the players than the effect the result might have on our supporters. Because of the fact that we had gone and beaten Holland and Germany, every team manager in the World Cup would now be watching for us when we set down in the United States.

That was fine. I could accept that as part of the warfare of football. But the heightened level of expectation among the Irish public would impose extra pressures on the players. At this point we can do without that.

Don't get me wrong. I'm a winner at heart, and from long years of experience as a player I realised more than most people what a victory over Germany really meant. We had just won a significant battle. But the war? That was something else!

Some weeks ago we had arranged that the players would have a three-day break with their families. It got them away from all the hype and settled them before our last warm-up game against the Czech Republic at Lansdowne Road.

To tell the truth, I was more delighted than any of them to be going home for a couple of days. I'd been away for the best part of a fortnight and with the exception of these few hours I wouldn't be setting foot in Newcastle again until mid-July.

The hype and the hustle and all the excitement of participating in the World Cup finals is fine. But there is a cost involved. When you've been living out of a suitcase for so long, you miss your wife, family, and not least, the grandchildren. It's hard to put a price on sacrifices like that.

The instructions were that the players would report back to Dublin on the Friday, but first I had another chore to perform. I had to go to Rome to watch Italy in action against Switzerland in one of their last appearances before meeting us.

Arrigo Sacchi, the Italian manager, was on record as saying that our win in Germany would cause him to revise his strategy, and I wanted to see exactly what he meant or if they were just empty words.

As it transpired, there were a couple of unusual features about the Italian display, but generally I felt I had seen it all before as they struggled to a 1-0 win over a Swiss team which has given them some real problems in recent years. I don't suppose there is ever a bad Italian team and this one looked strong and efficient. Yet I was not overly alarmed by what I saw.

I arrived back in Dublin on the Saturday night, and after checking out the fitness of the players with Maurice Setters, who had supervised two training sessions in my absence, I named a team. The first name down was Packie Bonner.

Packie, I gather, had won the first of his 73 caps in Poland on his 21st birthday. How appropriate it was that he should now smash Liam Brady's record on a ground where he had given Irish fans so many happy memories over the years.

I decided that this was an occasion to rest the Manchester United pair, Denis Irwin and Roy Keane, and that enabled me to try out a couple of things. I had been impressed by young Gary Kelly's displays at right-back and I wanted to take another look at him before we got to America.

With Keane out, I was able to revert to an orthodox 4-4-2 formation and bring back John Aldridge to partner Tony Cascarino in the front line. Aldo hadn't appeared in an Ireland shirt since the previous November and I knew that he couldn't wait for the chance to get back in and prove what he could do.

We had played with only one specialist striker in each of the previous three games and I was pleased with much of what I saw. I had promised, however, to examine all options, and in going back to 4-4-2 I was honouring that pledge.

Any time we are due to play a competitive game, I make a point of running the rule over the opposition. That normally doesn't apply in friendlies, and now I was going 'blind' into a meeting with a Czech team which some critics said had the makings of a good outfit.

Czechoslovakia had always produced good teams and at one point they were among the strongest footballing countries in Europe. I wasn't sure how the break-up of the old country would affect them now, but of one thing I was certain: they would be physically hard and technically correct.

A crowd of almost 44,000 turned up to say their goodbyes and that was a marvellous tribute to everybody. I wanted to do everything possible to deliver the result that they and I wanted. So I decided we would chase the game – and to hell with the consequences.

It involved, among other things, a licence for the two central midfielders, John Sheridan and Andy Townsend, to push forward without any firm commitment for one or other to anchor the line. It was a policy fraught with risk and the game wasn't very long in progress when it got us into trouble.

Paul McGrath (right) and Gary Kelly (below) in action against the Norwegians.

We've qualified for the last sixteen! Ronnie Whelan celebrates our emergence from the Group of Death.

The Czechs were a big strong team who didn't take any prisoners in the tackle, but ironically, it was the smallest player on the park, Martin Frydek, who gave us the most trouble. He operated just behind the front two, and with nobody picking him up he presented us with endless bother.

It was Frydek who forced Terry Phelan into conceding the penalty which enabled the Czechs to go in front early on in the game and it wasn't until a couple of minutes before half-time that we equalised. Tony Cascarino knocked down a cross by Steve Staunton and Andy Townsend's shot took a deflection on its way to the net.

In a normal situation, we would have dug in after that score and built methodically in search of a winner in the second half. But on this particular day we were committed to pushing players forward in numbers, and when you do that you are always liable to be caught on the break.

As I said, I didn't anchor anybody in the gap in front of the back four, but I still didn't reckon on the amount of space the opposition would have to run at the defence. That was a disappointment to me and inevitably it led to a situation in which Packie twice had to stoop to pick the ball out of our net. It was the first time in five games that we had conceded a goal and the fact that Packie was beaten three times made it faintly disturbing.

It was, of course, an unusual game in which I chose to dispense with the customary priorities, but I have to admit that I was disappointed with some of the individual performances, notably that of Paul McGrath. Against Germany, Paul had a smashing game, but this was quite different. He stood off his man, never made a decent tackle in the whole game and generally triggered off the alarm bells in me. I have it in mind to talk with him when we get to the States.

In the closing stages, I brought on Tommy Coyne for Tony Cascarino who had done well up to that point. Tommy might have had a couple of goals in the short time he was on, but in keeping with our performance on the day the ball stayed out and we were well beaten in the end.

Of all the ways to take our leave of our supporters, this was the worst. In the sense that it would help to take some of the pressure off us, I wasn't too depressed with the result. But I genuinely felt for the fans. As I've said time and again, they're the best in the world, and within minutes of the game ending they had buried their disappointment and the battle hymn of Olé! Olé! was ringing around the stadium.

That night we went to a charity dinner attended by the Taoiseach, Albert Reynolds, a charming man who entered into the spirit of the occasion. The autograph hunters, as usual, were there in numbers and I had to pinch myself when Mr Reynolds passed me on slips of paper from people looking for a signature. It's a great little country!

6 · June · 1994

This is the day the American adventure takes off – the day that we've all dreamed of for two years. I share the feeling of expectancy that has invaded millions of Irish people at home and across the world. The football, I know, I'll love but already, the thought of all those press, radio and television interviews and the thousand and one small things that are part and parcel of a manager's life during the World Cup finals, is already beginning to gnaw at me.

With no British team involved in the finals, I'm certain the media scrutiny is going to be even worse than in Italy four years ago and God knows, that was bad enough. Already, I wish I was on my way back from the tournament with a couple of good results under my belt.

The coach taking us from the hotel to Dublin Airport deposits us on the tarmac and as I look around, I can scarcely believe my eyes. There are literally thousands of people of all ages there, on every level of the building, some even on the roof. The goodwill is almost pouring down on top of us.

We've just lost to the Czech Republic less than 24 hours ago but you'd never guess it from the air of happiness and excitement in and around the building. Truly, our supporters are among the best in the world.

Inside the building, I meet up – again – with the Taoiseach, Albert Reynolds. This is the third time in as many weeks that I've been in his company so I say 'Mr Reynolds, we'll have to stop meeting like this'.

I unveil the logo for US '94 on the Aer Lingus plane taking us on the first leg of the journey to New York. I've noticed that there are only two engines on the plane – and I don't like crossing the Atlantic on anything with just two engines.

Maybe that's the reason the Aer Lingus people have decided to upgrade Maurice Setters and myself and a few of the FAI officials to first class. The lads are sat at the back of the plane and I take a bit of stick for that. But I can live with it!

There are a couple of hundred Irish supporters at New York to meet us but, unfortunately, they don't get to talk to the players. The airport authorities whisk us through a side exit and after a short coach journey we're on our way to Florida. The prospect of what I may find there worries me.

Our John, who does a bit of coaching in the States, has been to see the hotel in Orlando and he tells me – Dad, you're not going to like it. It's beside a five-lane highway and there are no walks available if anybody wants a stroll.

Now that bothers me. Because of the fact that I was ill at the time, I wasn't able to go to Florida to check out the facilities in February but Joe Delaney has been there and he assures me that our John is way off the mark.

According to him, it's about twenty minutes coach journey from both the training ground and the Citrus Bowl. And since we're only going to be using it at evening and night time, he reckons it's ideal. Me? I'll have to wait another half hour or so to find out.

Well, as it transpires, Joe has got it spot on and John's worries are groundless. The hotel is a good mile from the highway, there is enough privacy around the place for the players to go

We played
well against
Norway and
deserved
better than a
draw. Still, it
was enough to
get us to the
next phase,
and the fans
and the bench
all showed
their joy.

Of course, the Dutch match was a huge disappointment. We didn't play well in the first half, made silly errors and were punished for them. Roy Keane and Koeman fight for the ball.

The Dutch celebrate their passage through to the quarter-finals.

Homecoming. Andy and Kelly Townsend in the Phoenix Park.

walking and there's even a small lake where they can go and throw stones if they wish.

The hotel rooms are big and spacious and there's a bonus – each player has a room to himself. But you can't win them all and we're only in the place an hour or so when some of the younger players like Jason McAteer and Gary Kelly and a few of the older ones such as Dennis Irwin, inform me it's too lonely and that they would prefer to share. So I say fine, go and make your own arrangements.

We've got the top floor to ourselves, ensuring that they can have their privacy. I notice there's just one bar in the hotel – and that's another plus. It's easier to keep tabs on people when it's like that. They can go and visit the bar to do interviews and such like – but drinking alcohol is out. There are sufficient amusements like video games, pinball machines and card tables to keep them occupied without straying downstairs.

As soon as I reach the hotel, I'm off on those damn interviews with the press and I won't see my room for another couple of hours. When I get there, I find a lovely surprise. It's a beautifully appointed two-room suite with every convenience and there in the corner is a box, it seems, covered with cloth. When I examine it, I find it's a keg of the nicest Guinness you've ever tasted. I invite some of the press lads to the room and we sample the hospitality. Whatever about the weather, I think I'm going to enjoy this hotel.

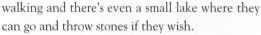

7 · June · 1994

I'm only out of the bed when I peer out the window. Instead of a blazing sun, the sky is overcast and it looks as if it's going to throw it down at any moment. And it does. Oddly enough, when we stepped off the plane last evening, I remarked to Maurice that it wasn't as hot as I had been led to believe. Were all those fears about heat and humidity so much hot air?

On the way to training, we go over the basic rules yet again. Any player with even the smallest strain will not be allowed take part in the ball work. We've still got the best part of a fortnight to go to our opening game against Italy, and in that situation, we're not going to take risks with anybody. But those players not involved in the mini game, will, of course, do their press-ups and upper body exercises just like everybody else. There will be no hanging about for anybody.

It's an ideal time, too, to remind them that if they choose to go for a walk in the evening, they do so in numbers. People walking alone, or with just one other person, can be at risk in these parts, and I'm not prepared to accept that responsibility.

This is precisely the same instruction as I issued in Italy four years earlier and they obeyed it. It is absolutely essential they now do so again so that we know precisely where they are at any given time.

The Seminole grounds will be our training base during our stay in Orlando. The grounds are well appointed, the changing facilities are good and there's a place where we can eat. There will be two sessions each day, two hours in the morning, a break for lunch at the ground and then back to work in the afternoon. It's going to be bloody hard work for everybody but if this is what it takes, this is what we'll give. It spills throughout the morning session, but it's not quite like rainy weather at home. The air is warm and you can train in comfort in it. But we didn't come to train in comfort. We're here to get ourselves in shape for some of the toughest conditions we'll ever experience and we want to be prepared for it.

The intake of liquid is very important and I stop the session every so often to allow the players to have a sip of water. But nobody can afford to take too much. People will be weighed at the end of each session and I want to have a reliable guide as to how they are sweating.

That's going to be the measure as to how they are adjusting to the heat and humidity, and unless the liquid intake is monitored carefully, we're not going to know where we stand.

We have a full lunch sent down by the people in our hotel, and soon it's back out for more work. Then, rather as I had feared, we pick up our first casualty. John Sheridan is already hobbling after being stood on during the Czech game, but now Kevin Moran has gone and tweaked a hamstring. I can do without this.

I tell Kevin to stop immediately and he does. After all we still have time on our side, and even if he misses the first game he has six days to get himself right for the next match with Mexico. At this stage I don't know if I'll be using him, but I want him fit and available if I need him.

When we get back to the hotel, I can sense the feeling of tiredness all round – and I'm pleased. We've started as we intend to finish, and after a seven o'clock dinner it's an early night for everybody.

8 · June · 1994

It's raining again this morning. Before we came out here, I'd been told that the sun, an unbelievably hot sun, shone all day and that thunderstorms broke over Orlando on the dot of five o'clock every evening. But we haven't seen the sun since we arrived and, thankfully, we've yet to experience a Florida thunderstorm.

All the way out to the training ground it's bucketing down, and I'm suddenly reminded that it was exactly the same when we went to Malta in 1990 to acclimatise for the heat in Italy. These programmes are all very nice and cosy when they're dreamed up back in Dublin, but the reality, as we're now discovering, can be something quite different.

If we had to go to America to prepare, why not Boston? That's a region with which we're quite familiar, and after visiting the city twice in recent years, we've a lot of good friends there. And while the rain in Florida may be warmer, it still interrupts sessions and prevents you pushing on with the job when it gets particularly heavy.

But those thoughts are born of frustration. In my heart of hearts I know that this is the place to be – if only the damn sun would come out and help us.

The first session goes along the usual lines, with warm-up exercises, upper body work and finally a game. These matches are competitive enough, but thankfully there's no Mick McCarthy out there to complicate things. Every time Mick tackled a player during training in

Italy I winced, but things are a little more sedate with this lot.

I'm particularly anxious to see how Paul McGrath is working out. Nobody has trained harder over this last couple of weeks than Paul, but I know and he knows that he's got a problem with his shoulder. Much as I would prefer it otherwise, he's now 'carrying' his damaged shoulder every time he moves, and already the prospect of the Italian match and the job he may have to do against Roberto Baggio with this kind of handicap is worrying me.

At the end of the session I make a point of going across and enquiring how he feels, and he's honest enough to tell me that there is still some restriction in his movement. But typical of Paul, he tells me not to lose any sleep over it – he'll be fine on the day.

John Sheridan doesn't train in the morning but he then informs me that he'll be ready to take a full part in the afternoon session. Somehow or other I knew it would come round to that. There's a hell of a lot more fun playing with a ball than squatting on the touchline doing exercises in the heat, and he's now champing at the bit to get fully involved.

We break for lunch and the players tell me that it's a waste of time and money having full lunches sent down to the ground when they have to be back out in half an hour and get down to more heavy work. So we decide that in future lunch will consist of just soup and sandwiches, and we'll wait until we get back to the hotel to have a full meal.

After dinner the lads go to the recreation room where Ray Houghton can show them yet again what an expert he is when it comes to a game of Scrabble. Andy Townsend, as ever, is willing to take on all comers at the snooker table, while many of them content themselves playing cards. There are a number of keen card players in the group, people like John Sheridan, Kevin Moran, Tony Cascarino and John Aldridge, but I don't think they make any fortunes on trips like this. The stake is no more than a couple of dollars – and I think they can just about afford that!

I get the first of the dinner invitations for World Cup managers, which tend to be thrown about like confetti at a wedding. The media people, press, radio and television, think that if they take you out for dinner, you'll give them some information out of the ordinary. But acceptance is fraught with some risk for the manager and unless the people involved are friends of mine, I decline. One thing I cannot afford to do on this trip is get offside with the media people by holding back on information for some, and dispensing it to others. Managers, you know, get wiser with the years.

9 · June · 1994

Yes, you've guessed it – more clouds and rain. This is becoming a bit of a joke. We've psyched ourselves for the bloody sun and all we get is wet, very wet. We might as well be back in Ireland – or England for that matter.

Still, we've got to be positive. And the good thing about it, if there is a good thing about it, is that it makes us push the lads that little bit harder to get the sweat out of them. It's easy enough to get a sweat on when the sun is

I had to take a last-minute phone call at the airport (above) just before leaving for America. Before that, of course, there was the inevitable press conference.

shining, but while the weather is still warm it needs a little extra energy to induce a real sweat. And in the long term, that's got to be good.

This will be a shortened working day. I've decided that we will again operate on a three-day cycle, with two hard days' work followed by a half-day off. The lads have run their butts off since we got here. They're now entitled to a little relaxation when we finish the morning session.

As usual there are a couple of hundred of our supporters already at Seminole when we get there, and I know that when the real action starts we're going to be able to count again on our secret weapon and outshout any opposition in the match stadiums.

The ground staff tell me there is a threat of a thunderstorm around and if it breaks while we're still out working, we're to get off the pitch immediately. Weather forecasting here is apparently pretty accurate, and the met. people are able to predict if there is lightning around, even when the cloud range is high and the threat is not immediately apparent to the casual onlooker.

Now, they take these things pretty seriously in Florida – and with good reason. Some of the mortality figures for lightning are frightening, and I'm directly responsible for the safety of twenty-two players and a back-up staff of anything up to ten people. I'll be guided by what the local experts tell me and if they say it's time to get indoors, we won't need any convincing.

Kevin Moran is still excluded from ball practice because of his injury, but John Sheridan appears to be moving without any problems. That is important, for while I still have an open mind on the team I'll send out against the Italians, I'm pretty certain, even at this stage, that John will be in it.

Dennis Irwin has had a couple of groin problems in recent weeks, but looking at him now, he seems to be in good shape. No less than Sheridan, he'll be in my plans for the first match. Dennis is one of the quieter members of the squad, but if he doesn't normally make his presence felt off the pitch, he's certainly very effective on it.

Like Roy Keane, he's had a long hard season with Manchester United and, ideally, I would prefer him to take things a little easier over the next week, but I suspect I'd be only wasting my breath. The players are keen to get on with it, and who am I to stop them?

The lunch-time press conference that day produces the first of the lurid stories that I had dreaded. Apparently one of the journalists has written in an article that there is a serial killer in the area and that he is stalking the Irish camp. Can you imagine that? Now, we may laugh these things off, but it's just possible that there is somebody at home, a friend or relative of one of the players, perhaps, who will take it seriously. So I ball the reporter out.

That afternoon, we have our first guided tour of the local amenities and we're brought to Universal Studios. People who had been there told me that some of the attractions were unbelievable, and having sampled them at first hand, I can vouch for that.

One of them, a film called *Back To The Future*, is so real that it would scare the living daylights out of you. The ride lasting five minutes, cost something like £13 million to make, but is calculated to make the hairs stand on the back of your neck. You don't move from your seat, but you'd never guess it as you head through ravines, plunge down into valleys, go to the edge of volcanoes, and generally die a thousand deaths. Bloody great stuff!

10 · June · 1994

The sun arrives at last, and while I'm dreading the effect it may have on the players, I'm glad it's here. After all, that is the main reason for our early arrival in Florida and if we're going to do well in this World Cup, we had better get used to it.

It is oppressively warm when we get to the park for training and I'm anxious to see how the lads run in it. It feels really hot – and I'm just standing there on the side-line barking out the instructions. Heaven knows how they're going to feel when they've been through an hour in this heat, but I'm pleasantly surprised.

Even the older fellows are holding nothing back and I marvel at the way people like Ray Houghton and John Aldridge are adapting to it. Ray knows he's under a bit of pressure to keep his place in the side, and he's responding to it in the only way he knows, putting himself about all over the pitch.

I'm interested also in how Ronnie Whelan is preparing. Although he hasn't been a regular member of the team all season, I was impressed by the way he responded when I asked him to do the anchoring job in midfield in the win over Holland in Tilburg.

Just now, that job is one of the biggest problems I'll have to tackle in selecting the team to meet Italy. There are three candidates for the position, Ronnie Whelan, Roy Keane and John Sheridan, and it's imperative that I make the right decision.

With the morning session finished, I hold the daily press conference, and when I get on the subject of liquid intake, one guy asks me how I'd react if the players wanted a beer or two. I said fine, that's OK providing it's authorised by management and controlled by management.

What I didn't comment on that day were my misgivings about the latest edict by FIFA, a copy of which had been dropped on my desk that morning. It concerned referees and FIFA's insistence that they clamp down on the tackle from behind. Such fouls, they said, should be punished with a red card, and failure to implement this directive would result in the match official being sent home.

Now, that worried me deeply on two counts. Firstly, I saw in the new interpretation of the tackle rule another move towards making football a non-contact sport, just as Michel Platini of France had advocated a couple of years earlier.

As a one-time defender myself, I regarded that as a retrograde step. Football was never meant to be a non-contact game. It's made up of many skills, one of which is the clean, decisive tackle. The way I view it, this new rule is designed to assist forwards. In the old days, the great attacking players earned their corn by learning how to beat the tackle. Our Bobby, for example, didn't become a great player by running through defences unopposed.

The other disturbing thing, of course, is the threat to referees that if they don't brandish red cards, they won't be doing their job properly. Now, what kind of carry on is that? How in heaven's name can refs go into games with an open mind and impart justice fairly and squarely if they're under that kind of blackmail? And that's what it is, for if they fail to carry out the directive they're not likely to be asked back in future years.

I'll tell you something. If I had my way, I'd use

The last thing we expected was rain in Orlando, but we got it.

The skipper relaxes after a training session.

▲ Cascarino goes highest. His injury was a big blow to us in America. It deprived us of one of our best weapons.

only those good match officials who are in their last year of service before retiring under the compulsory age limit. That way they could do the job without fear or favour and earn the gratitude of every player in the process.

I often wonder who these FIFA officials consult before changing the rules. Managers? Certainly not me! I've been in this job eight years and I've never once been requested to give an opinion on rule changes. And as far as I know, the same goes for other national team managers.

Anyway, we report back to work in the afternoon and get through another good session. Things are going well; the players are working hard and everything is on schedule. Immediately after training, we are taken to the Hard Rock Café in downtown Orlando and the lads enjoy a beer or two. It's non-stop rock music all the way – not my cup of tea – but clearly, some of the squad are impressed.

11 · June · 1994

I'm off today on the first of my travels. Mexico are playing Northern Ireland in a friendly game in New Haven, and seeing that we're playing the Mexicans in less than a fortnight, it's important that I get there.

As I've said before, friendlies are not the most reliable guide to a form – only the competitive games can give you a true read on a team – but since this will be the first look at the Mexicans for some time, the journey can be rewarding.

It will also be my first chance to meet up again with Bryan Hamilton who has taken over from Billy Bingham as Northern Ireland's manager. Bryan is an old friend of mine and I'm certain he'll do a good job for the IFA and build on the solid foundation which Billy left.

So I leave Maurice Setters to take charge of the training in Orlando and get an early morning flight north. The match goes pretty much as expected. When you get a team in the final stages of its World Cup preparations against a side which is at the end of its season, there is an obvious imbalance.

Northern Ireland played well at times, but in the end Mexico were worth their 3-0 win. They are a strong, skilful team with some outstanding individual players in key positions. Given that we must play them in the heat and humidity of Orlando, I'm already beginning to feel a little apprehensive.

Yet, it was less the game itself than an incident in the second half which really worries me. It was boiling hot in New Haven that day, and I couldn't believe my eyes when the referee refused to allow water bottles to be thrown on to the pitch to enable the players to take a drink.

This is bloody crazy. How do they expect players to run in those kinds of conditions for ninety minutes and not be allowed even a drink? Have they never heard of dehydration? I'll tell you something. There'll be serious damage done here over the next four or five weeks if FIFA persist in their refusal to listen to reason.

I look across at Bryan Hamilton and he can't believe it either. The difference is that in his case, it's just this once. Our lads are going to be in there for at least three games, and hopefully a lot more, and I intend to do everything in my power to ensure that they're not victimised.

When I get back to Orlando, I check with

Maurice as to how the training went. He tells me there have been no problems. Everybody, with the exception of Kevin and Tony, is fine; everybody is ready for the start of another heavy session the following morning.

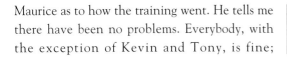

12 · June · 1994

We've arranged an impromptu game against a local college team today with the intention of giving our players ninety minutes of continuous work. The American lads come from just down the coast and while they may not have the skill of our players, the certainty is that they'll run just as hard. We can do with a good chasing at this point.

It's an unofficial game in the sense that I haven't asked an outside referee in to do the job. I want to be able to push players on and off during the match, and if you invite somebody to referee, he may tend to get a bit officious and make things awkward.

I want to be able to do it my way and make changes as I see fit. So I ask Steve, who is our liaison officer with the organising committee, to do the whistling. He knows his football and I ask him to award a few free kicks in and around both penalty areas, even if no foul has occurred, in order that we may practise our set piece moves.

Unfortunately Tony Cascarino will not be taking an active part, for he went and did some damage to the back of his leg yesterday. That's a setback, for with Niall Quinn out, Tony is the only big lad left up front.

At this point I'm not sure how bad the injury is, but the medical advice for Cass is to rest up and see how it comes along over the next week.

Kevin Moran, of course, is still out, but the rest are pretty well OK and I give them all a run at some stage.

The scoreline is unimportant, but I think we get it into double figures before the match is over. It's been a good exercise, and while nobody was on the pitch for the full ninety minutes, we fared pretty well in the heat.

Back in the hotel that evening, I notice that the media contingent is beginning to increase, with more people arriving by the day. There are more supporters about too, and things are building nicely for our first game, now only six days away.

One man who won't be there is Sean Connery, but I'm delighted to get a phone call from him, wishing us all the best in the Italian match. Sean, of course, is a Scot, but he tells me that he watched us against Italy in Rome four years earlier, and ever since he's been a fan of ours.

Earlier, I had received a good luck message from Senator Edward Kennedy. It's nice to have the good will of people like that. It also gave me the opportunity to deliver a nice little quote. When I mentioned the messages to a journalist, I told him: 'When I walk into that stadium with a Kennedy on one arm and James Bond on the other, nothing or nobody is going to stop me.' I liked that.

13 · June · 1994

Another bust-up with the media – and this time I'm raging mad. Remember that incident on Friday when the guy asked me if players could take the odd beer and I replied yes, providing it was authorised and controlled? Imagine my reaction then when I get word back from London that some of the tabloids have come out with headings like 'Carry On Boozing Says Jack'. Bloody crap! I never said any such thing. The fellow asked me a question and I gave him what I thought was a perfectly reasonable answer. And then I have to put up with rubbish like that!

When you've done it right and you know you've done it right, when the lads have worked their butts off and never once complained, that kind of stuff is hard to take. These players have been a credit to their team and to their country, and these kinds of scurrilous stories are undermining all that they're doing and all that they're about.

For the last four or five months, I've been telling the players to be on their best behaviour in the States. Since there are no British teams involved, all kinds of journalists will be honing in on them like bees around a honey pot, and they will be looking for all kinds of mud to sling.

I told them: 'The moment you err, they'll be on to you like a flash. You won't have to tell me about it – they will. The only problem is that they'll tell millions of others as well.' To be fair to the lads, they have been as good as their word in agreeing to pay heed to that request.

These journalists, whether they realise it or not, are undermining morale in the camp. And I'll do everything in my power to stop them. So, at lunch-time that day I read the riot act and I hope the people involved get the message.

Nor is that the only bone I have to pick with them. I also learn from friends back home that a report has appeared in a paper stating that Maurice Setters and Roy Keane had a stand-up row during training when I was away in New Haven.

I saw Maurice immediately and he seemed as astonished as I was. He said that he had done only what I had asked of him and worked the players hard. But he was adamant that there was no hard feeling or fall-out between Roy and himself.

At one point in the session he had shouted at the player to get a move on – no more, no less. Now I've been long enough in this business to know that when the No. 1 is away, players are tempted to take things a little easier than they would normally do. In a sense that's natural, but it's a long way from confirming that there was a bust-up between Maurice and Roy that day.

At the end of the press conference, I bring the two of them in and they tell it like it was – there was no dispute. I look around the room and I see a couple of sheepish faces.

Training in Orlando.

We're getting near the end of the hard work and I bet the lads thought the day would never come. We've done the graft, we've sweated in cloud and sun, and now we're as ready as we'll ever be to tackle the heat and humidity. From this on, it will merely be a case of topping up the tank and ensuring that bodies stay finely tuned.

According to my notebook – and theirs – it's Day 9 in the training camp, and we mark it with a game against the American Under-21 team. It's a little bit more formal than the one at the weekend, but the same rules apply. Joe McGrath, our senior coach, referees it, and he enters into the spirit of things by letting play develop and, of course, we make loads of substitutions.

Eventually we win 4-2 with the help of a couple of goals from David Kelly, but that is relatively unimportant. The significant thing is that the players are now moving quite easily in the heat, and with just a couple of exceptions – Steve Staunton is the most notable – they've come to terms with the conditions.

Steve has blond hair and a fair complexion, and I suppose if anybody was going to suffer out here, it was he. It troubles me, but with his great competitive spirit I hope that eventually he'll come to terms with it.

That reminds me of one of the great talking points in my life just now – water bottles. The latest from FIFA is that players can take water, once they step off the pitch. But what kind of a directive is that?

It's all very well for the wide players to step over the side-line, but what about the central players. How are they going to get to the line while the game is in progress.

Or, perhaps, the powers that be wish us to take lads off on a rota basis and play with just ten at any one time. It would be laughable if it weren't so serious.

If players are not allowed to take liquid, they'll dehydrate in this weather. And if they dehydrate seriously, they are liable to die. Are the authorities still adamant that the risk is justifiable? Or are they ready to pass the buck on to somebody else.

The news of our casualties is that Kevin Moran is coming along nicely, but it looks as though Tony Cascarino will not be in the frame for Saturday's game. He's still feeling the pull in his leg, and at this rate he'll struggle to be ready for the second game against Norway.

Niall Quinn, like Mark Lawrenson, joined in the preliminary work this morning, and it was a reminder to me of what might have been. Mark was forced to quit through injury at a time when he still had so much to give to the team in 1988. He was a profound loss.

Niall is of more recent vintage, of course, but as a result of that unfortunate knee injury, he's here now purely as an onlooker. I can imagine just how he feels as he watches his mates prepare, but if it's any consolation to him, we feel the loss just as much.

15 · June · 1994

Today it's the turn of the television people to get a talking to. During my altercation with some of the written press yesterday, they filmed the scene at the press conference, and as I said my piece I'm sure it didn't make for pretty viewing back home.

Now, these television people, as I saw it, were basically dishonest. They turned up with their cameras at the press conference even though they had ample opportunity to do their thing at other times.

After the conference had started, they walked away from the cameras and, naturally, I assumed that they weren't working. But I was wrong. What they did was leave the cameras on, filming everything that happened in the room. I was being deceived. There and then I determined that as soon as the conference started, the red lights were to be switched off, and we conducted the session without the prying eyes of the lens.

I had another go at television personnel later in the day, this time at those working for Sky Sports. Together with the players, I had contracted with ITV, BBC, RTE and UTV, that in return for my co-operation during the World Cup I would receive a certain sum. The players had a similar agreement, but when approached, Sky Sports refused to be party to it.

And yet, they keep turning up day after day, looking for interviews with either the players or myself, and sometimes both. Now, so many cameras are stuck in front of me that it's hard to keep tabs on who's who. But today I spotted Sky Sports and promptly refused to do a piece for them. Then, this fellow tells me that they are prepared to pay me and says there will be a fee of

£50 on offer. And I say to him, don't talk daft.

The camera crews and journalists involved get frustrated – and rightly so. The people who should be on the mat are the decision-makers back home who refuse to pay up and yet expect the crew to get around to do their stories.

There are those, I suspect, who will accuse us of greed, but that doesn't wash with me. For a few short weeks, the players are among the most important people in the world, and I believe that they are entitled to maximise their earnings from that.

They have worked like slaves for four years and got relatively little. They didn't lose a game and yet missed out on the bonuses that were going for qualification for the 1992 European championship in Sweden. Now players generally get what they're worth – in some cases they are paid more than they're worth.

But our lot are no ordinary players. They are among the best in the game, and people like Roy Keane, Andy Townsend, Paul McGrath, Ray Houghton and Steve Staunton are recognised as such. They're worth every penny they're paid and I say fair play to them. We read in the papers of golfers like Bernhard Langer and Nick Faldo signing million pound club contracts. Do people also accuse them of being avaricious?

No, our lads are getting only what they deserve and, after all, they only enter into deals which are acceptable to both sides. So, it annoys me to hear stories which smack of begrudgery.

Out on the training park, I have a bit of a go today at Roy Keane. I look across at one stage and notice that he is just standing there doing nothing. When I ask him if he has a problem, he tells me that he has a bit of a groin strain. More than that, he informs me that he's had it for a couple of days – and I see red.

I ask him if he's heard me preaching over and over again that if anybody has an injury problem, they don't train. There are still four days to go to the Italian match – we don't need to risk anybody in training, particularly in his case after the kind of season he's had at Old Trafford.

He tells me that he intends to run it off, and I inform him that he'll run off nothing of the kind. He'll stop there and then, and if he doesn't he's in big trouble. Now Roy is not the easiest person to deal with. He's basically a shy lad who will never volunteer conversation, and unless you approach him, you'll learn nothing. But on this occasion at least I think he takes the point.

16 · June · 1994

We're up at 7 a.m. to catch a flight to New York – much too early. After all, we're travelling on a charter and presumably we could have left any time it suited us. So why get us up at that hour? Still, that's what our itinerary says and we'll stick to it.

Our base for the two games in Giants Stadium in New Jersey will be the Sheraton Tara Hotel in Parsippany, some twenty miles or so outside New York. It's close enough to the stadium to obviate the risk of long delays on our way to and from matches, and yet sufficiently removed to keep us detached from the hype now building up around Saturday's game.

The building itself could scarcely be more impressive, a castle-like structure which fills the eye as you approach it. The suite I will share with Maurice Setters during our stay here is fit for a king.

Among the facilities is one of the best-filled drinks cabinets you're ever likely to see. Every conceivable drink is there, but I'm not sure at first whether it's a pay bar or a complimentary one. Eventually I discover that the drinks are on the house, so that will give me an opportunity to have a few friends in for a social night.

Since all the graft is now behind us, there will be no training today. Instead, the programme comprises a talk-in on match strategy and an analysis of the Italian team we are likely to face in just over forty-eight hours time.

A couple of weeks ago, I went to Rome to watch Italy play Switzerland in a match which I felt would provide a valuable line to the current strengths of both teams. Now, my normal practice is to jot down notes on team patterns: the way they play and the key individuals involved.

What I do is write down numbers and then match them later with the names on the game programme. Because of the pressures of the last couple of weeks, I haven't had a chance to do so on this occasion, and therefore I have to refer to numbers rather than names.

This, for some reason or other, causes amusement among the players, and as I'm talking, I hear a few sniggers. I immediately see red. I tell them that I've given up two days of my time to go and check players out for their benefit, put up with all the hassle of travel, and now they're not even paying attention.

'You bloody listen and listen well,' I tell them.

Even then, I notice a few people looking over my shoulder at the telly behind me, and that makes me even more angry. We're only two days away from the game and, damn it, I expect more than this. So I go on the warpath again and this time they get the message.

It will be another early night for everybody, but even as I'm hanging about, killing time, I settle in my mind the last outstanding problems about my team for Saturday. I'll not tell the players until training tomorrow. But I figure I've wrestled long enough with whether to follow my instincts or go with logic.

I'll side with instinct and place my trust in the players who have been through this kind of warfare before. And that means that I'll go with Dennis Irwin and Ray Houghton down the right flank.

It is just possible that Gary Kelly and Jason McAteer could do a better job for me, but that would be to gamble unduly. At this stage of the ball game, I'm not prepared to do that.

Ray has worked harder than ever in his career to keep his place, and dedication like that deserves to be rewarded. Dennis, too, has looked sharp in training, and while Alan Kernaghan has claims to a place in central defence, I'll settle for a partnership of Paul McGrath and Phil Babb.

Roy Keane will fill the 'hole' in midfield, leaving John Sheridan and Andy Townsend to do the play-making; and despite the claims of John Aldridge, I reckon Tommy Coyne's impressive display of non-stop running against the Germans was good enough to earn him his place.

So that's it then – the most important decision I've made since arriving in the States. I'll hold on to my secret for a few hours longer, but I bet there are a lot of people out there who would love to share it.

17 · June · 1994

We have the opportunity of training in Giants Stadium at match time, which is 3.30 p.m., but I decline in favour of a morning session. I prefer to get the players up early, get them breakfasted and on the coach for 10.30 a.m.

This is our first sighting of the famous stadium and it lives up to its reputation. It is a huge, three-tiered arena, and as I walk the pitch I can imagine what it will be like tomorrow when there will be almost 77,000 fans in those stands.

The training session lasts only an hour and it consists of nothing more than light jogging with only a minimum of ball work. The important thing is to give the lads a feel of the place, let them get to know their bearings, so that it won't seem all that strange when they walk out there tomorrow.

In keeping with custom, I give them the team as we're chatting on the pitch. There is no dissention – there never is – but I reckon I may have heard a sigh or two of relief.

Soon it's time for them to be back on the coach while I go to do my press conference. As I'm walking to the conference room, somebody presses a slip of paper into my hand, and to my surprise I discover it's the Italian team selection.

I glance through it and the names seem to

 Packie Bonner in training prior to the Italy game.

jump off the paper. Most of these players are held in awe in our part of the world, and here we are about to go to war with them for the three points which would go a long way towards ensuring our survival to the knock-out stages of the championship.

The points which strike me immediately are that Arrigo Sacchi, the Italian manager, is going against the norm by playing Roberto Donadoni on the right side of midfield and, more controversially still, he's opted for a 4-4-2 formation, with Roberto Baggio and Giuseppe Signori playing up front.

Collectively, Baggio and Signori are worth their weight in gold, but it's not like the Italians to shed a sweeper to play two strikers in a game of this importance. That suggests to me that Sacchi is still torn by self-doubt about his best formation – all very encouraging.

For the remainder of the day, we just hang around the hotel doing nothing but conserving energy. I advise the lads to go and lie on their beds, put their feet up and do as little as possible. They'll need all their energy and more to cope with the Italians in this kind of heat.

From my own playing days, I know only too well how difficult it is for players to relax the day before a big game. And maybe that's the reason I wandered into one of the bedrooms around 11 o'clock before going to my own room.

I don't normally check on players in this manner. They're all adults; they know as well as I do that they must have their quota of sleep and they're sensible enough to take this on board. Perhaps it's a sign of my own nerves that I'm now breaking my own rules, but in fact there is nothing out of place. They're playing cards and video games, and soon the corridor is deathly quiet. Like me, they'll go to sleep with the names of eleven Italian players on their minds.

18 · June · 1994

A troubled night – and it has nothing to do with the Italians. The phone in my room rings in the dead of night and when I look at my watch, I find it's still only four o'clock. It's a journalist from India who keeps calling me sir. Tell me about the names of your players, sir; tell me about your game tomorrow, sir.

Now, my first reaction is to bung down the phone, but I ask him: 'Do you know what time it is here?' I tell him to call me at nine in the morning and yes, you've guessed it, he rings me on the dot, with the same silly questions.

In all, I get four calls during the night, three of them from people in Ireland wishing me well. I don't know them from Adam, but while I'm glad of their support, this is hardly the time to deliver it. In future, I'll instruct the hotel staff not to put any calls through to my room after midnight.

Because of the afternoon kick-off, there is going to be a lot of time to kill, and the majority of the lads skip breakfast in favour of brunch around 11.30 a.m. As soon as that's over, we go for a bit of a stroll as we always do on big match days.

I find this invaluable. It gets us away from the noise and hype in the hotel lobby and gives us a few quiet minutes just to be alone with ourselves and our thoughts. Then, it's back to bed for everybody and I manage to doze off for half an hour or so before Mick Byrne calls to get us up and on the road.

We follow the usual format. Charlie O'Leary, who is in charge of the tapes on the coach, plays some stirring Irish ballads to get us in the mood for the job ahead. Along the way we pass thousands of Irish fans heading for the stadium. Whatever else, we're not going to lack vocal support.

The instruction to the players is to do their warm-up exercises inside in the dressing room. It's far too hot to do even the lightest work in a temperature close to 90 degrees, and apart from walking up to the half-way line and back just to sample the atmosphere, we stay indoors.

I talk to them collectively for a few minutes, then go round and speak with them individually, advising them what they may expect and, equally important, what we expect of them. I tell them to get as much liquid as possible into them but not too much at one time. They're going to lose a lot of body fluid out there and it is vitally important that they sip liquid regularly between now and kick-off time.

I'm struck by the fact that they're all very composed. Some are plugged into cassettes, others are chatting quietly among themselves while Mick Byrne does his strappings. Then the FIFA man comes in, gives us our instructions and tells us that when the bell goes, we have two minutes to exit the dressing room.

An hour later, he's back and neither of us is impressed. He tells me that we're wearing the wrong strip and he gives us two minutes flat to get it off and get kitted out again. I'm absolutely livid. I point to the fact that we've been instructed, not once but twice, to wear white shirts, green togs and white stockings.

He argues that we've got it wrong, that the Italians are kitted out in white, blue and white. Now, on occasions like this, you take three sets of kits to the stadium, the one you intend to wear, a reserve set and one which goes to charity. The last thing I want now is this kind of situation; but rather than argue with him, I tell the lads to change.

All the while, the Italian players are standing outside in the tunnel and they're not amused. It means that we're two or three minutes late walking out, but in the waves of excitement now rolling across the ground, I'm sure very few people notice it apart from ourselves.

Giants Stadium is an imposing place when it's empty; now with row after row of spectators reaching half-way to the sky it seems, it is positively awe-inspiring. My understanding is that the teams will be presented to dignitaries before the kick-off, and in the expectation that they will be standing about in the heat for anything up to ten minutes, I get white caps without advertising material for the players to wear, to protect their heads from the sun.

As it transpires the pre-match ceremonies are mercifully short, but the atmosphere when the crowd sings the two national anthems is something else. The Italians are good but our lot win hands down.

Then, almost before we realise it, the game is on. The early minutes are always nerve-racking on days like this, but I'm pleasantly surprised with the way we're handling things now. We're getting at them just as much as they're worrying us, and apart from one incident involving Paul McGrath, we get through the first ten minutes without any alarms.

Dino Baggio played a long ball through for his namesake to chase, and for one dreadful second

Kevin Moran was
the old man of the
squad. Seen here
in the win against
Holland at
Tilburg, he didn't
play in America
but he was always
there to provide
vital cover at the
heart of the
defence if needed.

Roy Keane and
Baggio jump
together in the
great win against
Italy.

it looked as if Paul wasn't going to get there ahead of him. But he did, just in the nick of time and we all breathed easily again.

Then all hell breaks loose, and suddenly we're on our feet like schoolboys, hugging and kissing each other. A bad clearance by Franco Baresi falls nicely for Ray Houghton and as he bears in from the right, I think he's going to play the ball wide to Stephen Staunton. Instead, he swings his left leg at it, and with goalkeeper, Pagliuca, yards off his line, he puts just enough pace on the shot to get it up and down with inch-perfect judgment.

Now, I've seen that kind of lob shot tried a million times. Too often, it has glanced off the crossbar and back into play. But as I'm standing there watching Ray's effort, as if in slow motion, I shout, 'Bloody hell! This one's going in.' And it did.

A glance at the clock in the stadium tells me that we've only been playing 13 minutes and my first thought, incredibly, is 'We've gone and scored too early. There's a whole bloody game to get through yet. They're bound to come back even stronger at us.'

But, of course, that's a silly thought. We've got a start that none of us could ever have dreamed about. Even if the Italians score now, we'll still get a point. And, to be brutally honest, I'd have settled for that before the game.

Ray is forever trying to lob the goalkeeper in practice and never once have I seen him succeed. Now he's gone and done it on this day of days and I'm thrilled for him. For nobody has sweated more just for the privilege of playing in the game.

Looking at the teams, you'd never guess that we were the underdogs. Phil Babb is playing brilliantly at centre-back, the two full-backs, Dennis Irwin and Terry Phelan are settling nicely and knocking in some good balls, and

generally there is an assurance about our play that bodes well for the result.

Then looking at the clock I discover that we've gone 25 minutes, and the thought strikes me that our lads haven't yet had a drink of water. I roar at the referee, indicate that the lads need a drink, but he just poo-poohs me away. Finally, there is a short stoppage down in the corner and the wide players, people like Irwin and Houghton on our side and Phelan and Staunton on the other wing, are able to have a drink.

But there's no such luxury for the central players. They can't take time out to come to the line for the simple reason that the game may restart at any moment. They represent my main engines and they haven't had a drop of water since the match started. And still, the referee refuses to facilitate them.

Eventually, we get to half-time and I walk directly to the referee with a water bottle in my hand to indicate my concern. But as I get to him, I realise that there's no point in talking to this prat. So I hand him the bottle, and he proceeds to drink from it. So much for my protest!

Instead of sitting on the benches, the players lie on the floor during the half-time break, sipping liquid slowly and replenishing their fluid levels. We've done well to this point, and hopefully we can keep it going until we get to the end.

In fact, there are remarkably few moments of stress in our penalty area in the second half. Roberto Baggio has a snap shot which brings a fine reflex save from Packie Bonner, and later, Dennis Irwin produces a good tackle to stop the same player. Given the circumstances, he had to be spot on in his timing of the tackle but, no less than Babb later in the game, he showed that he had the nerve to handle the situation.

The referee, who has booked both Irwin and Phelan, is still doing us no favours, and when I go to substitute McAteer for Houghton, he simply looks away. Ironically, while we're still arguing the point on the side-line, Ray almost scores a second time.

The ball breaks out to him at the angle of the penalty area and he catches it full on the instep. Given that there are three or four players in front of him, Pagliuca does well to see it coming through and pulls off a fine save at the foot of the upright.

That might have wrapped it up for us, but it doesn't compare with the chance just a few minutes later when Roy Keane, sparing nothing or nobody in these cruel conditions, gets in behind the defence down the left and lays the ball back for John Sheridan.

Of all the players on the pitch, I would back John to put it away in that situation, but he leans back just a shade too much and instead of finishing in the top corner of the net, the ball hits the crossbar. That was by far the best chance of the game and by missing it we give ourselves unnecessary hassle in the last ten minutes.

In fact the referee allows the game to go on for 94 minutes, but it is perhaps a measure of the way I'm caught up in it, that I don't notice until he blows time up, and victory, sweet victory, is ours. We've gone and done what the critics said

was impossible, and for the first time in eight meetings of the countries, we've beaten Italy.

I walk to Arrigo Sacchi, tell him that I expect Italy to win their next two games, and I'm just about to leave the pitch when I notice the police manhandling two of our supporters on the pitch. They've just run on to congratulate the players and while they're out of order in doing that, I'm incensed by the way they're being treated.

So I tell the police: 'By all means arrest them, but do it sensibly. There are 20,000 of our supporters out there watching you and they'll not stand by and see these two lads abused.' The cops get the message and take them off quietly.

Of all the occasions we've celebrated success in our dressing room, this is one of the best. We couldn't have asked for a better way to kick off our programme. Now, the sky's the limit.

I'm staying in New Jersey overnight before leaving for Washington in the morning to watch Mexico play Norway. The players return immediately after the game to Florida, and by the time they get there, they won't be in much mood for celebration.

The word from Dublin is that the people are out on the streets celebrating, and that makes the day even better. Me? I have a quiet meal in the hotel with my wife and with no supporters around to share our sense of happiness. I'm in bed by eleven o'clock. Still, it's been some day!

19 · June · 1994

A long, long day starts with a taxi ride to Newark Airport for a scheduled 7 a.m. flight to Washington. With me are Des Casey and an old friend, David McBeth, who has come over from England to support us.

The problem is that we're seated on the plane for almost an hour waiting for a spare part to arrive, and I don't like being in a confined space for that length of time. I'm just about to ask to be allowed to leave the plane when the captain comes on to tell us all to disembark.

We don't hear the call to get back on board thirty minutes or so later and the upshot is that they're about to close the doors when we happen to saunter down to the designated gate in the departure lounge. As things turn out, it might have been better if they had.

On the drive in from Washington Airport we stop off at Arlington Cemetery and like thousands and thousands of other visitors pay our respects at the grave of John F. Kennedy. The city, it seems, is full of Mexican supporters and when we check in for lunch at a downtown restaurant, they recognise me. Word of our win over Italy has travelled fast.

The seats we have place us in the VIP area in the RFK Stadium, not a thousand miles from where the man himself, Dr Joao Havelange, the President of FIFA, is seated. If he recognises me, he certainly doesn't show it, but I'm not greatly bothered. The person next to me is the Minister for Sport in Norway, a woman who has some enlightened comments to make on the game.

Twenty-four hours earlier, we had suffered in the intense heat in New Jersey, but if anything it's even worse here in Washington. It doesn't bother the Mexicans, of course, but pity those poor Norwegians having to run and chase for ninety minutes in these conditions.

On one occasion, they actually stopped to run over to the line for drinks and were almost made to pay the penalty. The Mexican goalkeeper immediately humped the ball upfield, and those same players had to scamper back to prevent the Mexicans running through unopposed. As I'm silently contemplating Norway's ordeal, I look at the FIFA dignitaries seated around me. At regular intervals a hostess comes along and offers us iced drinks. And on two occasions, once in either half, they come around with chilled napkins for us to place on our heads.

As the unfortunate Norwegians continue to suffer, I turn and say to Des: 'Damn it to hell, but who are these people to put the safety of players on the line while they sit around in the lap of luxury with their iced drinks and chilled napkins. It's just not right and I will continue to rant on about it.'

The FIFA man in Orlando tells me that I'm the only one kicking up a fuss about water bags and implies that I should join other managers in their silence. My answer is that they're silent only because I'm out there in front doing the shouting for them.

For all their problems with the weather, Norway are doing extraordinarily well. They will never be accused of over-stretching their limitations, but what they do, they do well. And when the opposition have the ball, they certainly get players back in numbers.

Mexico, on the other hand, strike me as a very useful team going forward, with a couple of players of exceptional skill. And they can defend a bit too, as they show on those occasions when Jan Fjortoft puts them under pressure.

Overall, the Mexicans look the more likely side to win, but the game is still scoreless when we decided to leave five minutes or so before the end to beat the crowds and catch our air connection back to Florida. We have just reached the gate when a huge roar goes up, obviously to acclaim a goal.

So we rush back up the steps, fully expecting to see the Mexicans celebrating. Imagine our surprise then when, on reaching the top of the stairs, we find it is the Norwegians who have scored – and are now odds-on to win.

It proves that their wins over England and Holland in the preliminaries were no flukes, but in a way it is possibly the wrong result for us. It's going to fire the Mexicans up still more for next Friday's game in Orlando – and that's not a reassuring prospect in the heat and humidity of Florida.

We make the airport on time, only to discover that because of a bad electrical storm all flights are either deferred or cancelled. Eventually I am offered a seat on a plane going to Charlotte and I take it, in the hope that I may be able to make a connection there which will get me to Orlando.

But that proves a forlorn hope, and with no hotel accommodation available in the city, I spend the night sitting on a hard, plastic chair in the airport. Don't ever talk to me about the glamour of international football or the joys of managing a team in the World Cup.

20 · June · 1994

When I eventually make it back to the team hotel this morning, I need only one thing – sleep. So I go to my room with specific instructions that I don't wish to be awakened until four o'clock.

When I eventually surface, the news is not very good. I learn for the first time about Tommy Coyne's ordeal after the Italian match. On top of that, Andy Townsend's knee is up like a balloon and things are not looking good for Friday's crunch match with Mexico.

Coyne's ordeal merely substantiates all the fears I had voiced about players being put at risk by lack of body fluid. I hold up my hand and say that, in hindsight, I ought to have substituted him earlier than I did, and to that extent I contributed to the problem.

But the fact remains that he was one of those players who found it impossible to get a drink during the game. The painful evidence was there if FIFA chose to notice it when he had to be wheeled on and off the plane taking the squad back to Florida on the night of the game.

To make matters worse, he was one of the two Irish players required to provide a urine sample when the game finished, at a stage when he was quite obviously in an advanced state of dehydration. There he sat, still togged out for some three and a half hours while he gulped down liquid in the hope of producing the sample.

That merely induced a state of dizziness, a kind of water drunkenness, and the fact that nobody told him he could shower until he was into the second hour of his ordeal merely pointed up the insensitivity of officialdom. One way or another, it was an eventful day for Tommy, who had been brave to a fault in his preparedness to run and run.

Early in the second half, he was deliberately elbowed in the head by an Italian player, and when he refused to get on to a stretcher to be carted off to the side-line, he was shown a yellow card. Now what kind of justice is that?

Apart from anything else, how could I or any other manager be certain that the stadium attendants moving a player with a head injury on to a trolley were qualified to do so, and would not exacerbate the damage? Surely the final

◀

Andy
Townsend
led from the
front in the
Italian
victory.

arbiter in a situation like that should be the team doctor.

Andy's knee problem is more mysterious. The initial diagnosis is that he is suffering from poison ivy, brought on by the fact that he apparently leaned against an ivy fence as the players enjoyed an after-match drink in New Jersey.

I've just seen his knee and it doesn't look particularly hopeful. Both his legs are covered with a rash, and his infected knee is almost twice the normal size. I intend to get him to a city hospital to see a dermatologist in the morning. It's just as well there are another five days to go to the Mexican match.

For the remainder of the players, the orders are to put their feet up and get as much energy as possible back into their bodies by Friday. They had a free day yesterday when they were joined by their wives and families, which was the least they deserved. There will be no more hard training sessions between this and match day.

21 · June · 1994

Another free day for the players. Instead of subjecting them to running and ball work, I believe they can benefit more from a day at the beach, so I organise a coach tour to Cocoa Beach which is just outside Cape Canaveral.

We arrive there at around noon and the players are free to do as they choose for the next three hours or more. I tell them to watch out for the jelly fish if they go for a swim, and if they want a drink or two, that's fine by me.

The odd man out in all of this, of course, is Andy Townsend. He's gone to the hospital for another examination of his knee, and the consensus is that the problem has been brought on, not by contact with ivy but by a tin of insecticide which the players were given to guard against mosquito bites.

Alan McLoughlin used the same spray and ended up with a rash on his chest. The specialist agrees with our own medical experts, Martin Walsh and Conal Hooper, that the allergy should clear by Friday, but it could be a race against time.

When we get back to the team hotel, Sean Connolly informs me that I've won my case. When I ask him what he means, he produces a fax message from FIFA stating that from here on in, water bags can be thrown to players on the pitch.

Now, that's all I ever asked of the officials in the first instance, and it seems crazy to me that it took them so long to see reason. Given the experience of the games in New Jersey and Washington, I think that it is only right and proper, but I can't help wondering if this isn't victory at a price.

I've now publicly criticised FIFA on at least two counts – and I don't suppose they like it. Back at the start of our stay here, I took issue with Dr Havelange and his ultimatum that if referees didn't send players off for tackles from behind, they themselves would be sent home. Now, that kind of statement from a man in his position was out of order – and I felt justified in attacking it.

Then, of course, there was the water bag issue which has just been resolved. I don't imagine that I'm FIFA's favourite manager at the moment.

All the while, I'm thinking about my line-up for the game on Friday and, in particular, the choice of a man to lead the attack. Tommy Coyne is recovering well from his ordeal of last Saturday, but I'm still uncertain if the timescale is right for him to play.

John Aldridge and David Kelly are both champing at the bit for a chance to get on, but one player definitely out of the running is Tony Cascarino. His recovery rate from the calf muscle injury sustained during the first week of our stay here is very slow, and at this point I'm not very optimistic about his chances.

When he got the injury in the first place, he informed me that it was at the back of his leg. But now I notice that he is being treated much further down his leg – an ominous sign. At this point, I don't see Cass playing much of a part in the championship.

22 · June · 1994

This is the day when we make our acquaintance with the dreaded Citrus Bowl Stadium in Orlando. Even before we set down here, local experts were predicting that it would be one of the most difficult of all match venues in use for the championship because of the oppressive heat and humidity of Florida at this time of year.

There was a time back in the first week of our pre-championship training when those fears appeared to me to be overstated. That was when the cloud ceiling was low and we went for three full days without seeing the sun.

But that situation has long since changed, and by now we've become accustomed to seeing the sun shine out of a cloudless sky in the first half of the day. We must walk out on Friday for a noonday kick-off with a team thoroughly familiar with these kinds of conditions.

In the normal course of events you are not permitted to train at the match venue until the day before a game, but that stipulation doesn't apply here. Holland and Belgium are scheduled to play in Orlando the day after our game with Mexico, which means that training arrangements for all four teams have been brought forward by twenty-four hours.

When we get to the Citrus Bowl, we discover it is a huge horseshoe-shaped stadium capable of accommodating more than 70,000 spectators. And to judge by the demand for tickets, it seems as if it may still not be big enough to satisfy the demand.

My first impression is that it is not as bad as I had been led to believe. The open space at one end of the ground permits a flow of cool, refreshing air, or at least air that is not stifling. It was boiling hot when we first got here, but then a bit of a breeze blew up and I said to the lads: 'Hey, this may not be as bad as we feared.'

But then somebody pointed out that there was a lot of cloud about and that was distorting the picture. It is almost certain that when we turn up on Friday it will be 100 degrees in the shade,

Jason McAteer gets the better of Paolo Maldini.

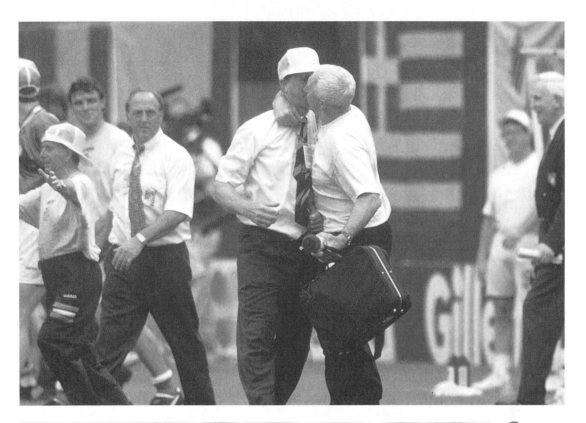

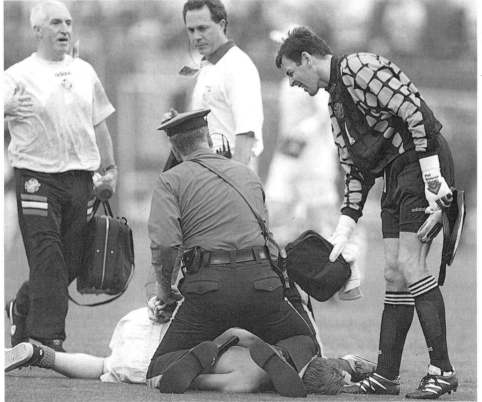

Mick Byrne can't contain himself at the end of the Italian match (above) while Packie Bonner tells an over-zealous policeman to go easy on one of our fans.

with no wind to offer the slightest hope of respite.

As was the case in Giants Stadium, the playing surface here in Orlando is absolutely superb. Whatever else, the Americans know how to prepare pitches, but what a pity it will all be ripped up once this tournament is over.

Back in the team hotel we watch a video of Mexico's game against Norway and it confirms my original impression about the Mexicans. They are a slick, well-organised side with a lot of pace. We've got to impose ourselves on them in midfield and ensure that they don't have the opportunity of running at our defence.

The swelling on Andy Townsend's knee has reduced considerably and I reckon he will be ready to join us in light training tomorrow. That's a relief, for apart from his leadership qualities, he gives us a real physical presence in midfield and we may need that more than ever now.

I'm still looking at Paul McGrath's shoulder and still worrying. Clearly, the man is restricted in his movement, but considering the way he performed against Italy last Saturday, there is no way I can afford to leave him out, even in his present state.

That, I suspect will mean a further disappointment for Alan Kernaghan who is sitting around waiting for his big chance. He's looked as good as anybody in training, but it's hard to change a winning side.

I'll sleep on the problem for another night and then commit myself to a selection tomorrow. But there is no way I'll make it public until such time as the Mexicans name theirs. And right now it looks as if they intend to persist in their game of cat and mouse until match day.

23 · June · 1994

I have another go at Roy Keane this morning. He was one of the players in the 'wars' in the Italian match, for he finished it with what we in the trade call a 'dead' leg. And when you think of the way he played in New Jersey and the enormous workrate he produced in the conditions, that wasn't altogether surprising.

Ever since that match, the lads have been on the easy list, but short of putting a harness on him, how can I stop Roy running? The lad, it seems, is born to run, and while that is a huge advantage to any manager who has charge of him, it can also cause problems.

Like now. As those of you at home watching our games on television will no doubt have noticed, he's had his hair shaved tight in what, I can only surmise, is his latest concession to fashion. Now here he is, out in the scorching sun with no headgear on, charging about when he's supposed to be resting his leg.

So I call him in and give him a piece of my mind. And guess what? Within another five minutes, I spot him out on an adjoining pitch, whacking balls in at Packie Bonner. I might have known Packie would be involved, for no matter what I say, both he and Alan Kelly will insist on running and throwing themselves about in training.

But Roy and his dodgy leg is a different matter. I desperately need him to be fit

◀
Jason
McAteer
really came
of age in
America.

tomorrow, and yet here he is putting the whole thing at risk. Now, whether he forgets what I say to him or deliberately lets it in one ear and out the other, I don't know, but he gets my dander up at times.

So I say to Maurice Setters: 'Go and tell him that unless he's back in here in the shade inside two minutes, he's out of the team tomorrow.' I don't know what Maurice said to him but I notice they're both having a big laugh as they leave the pitch and retire into the shade.

Before we leave the training ground, I give the lads the team. And for all the soul-searching of the last few days, I don't think it surprised any of them. I've had a word with Tommy Coyne and he assures me that he's feeling fine and looking forward to the game. Armed with that information, I'll put him in the side and keep Aldo in reserve.

I've also spoken with Paul and his reaction was predictable enough. He informs me that his shoulder is better and that he'll be fine. Phil Babb is an automatic choice alongside him and in spite of the claims of Gary Kelly and Jason McAteer, I'll go again with Dennis Irwin and Ray Houghton down the right flank.

I'm a bit concerned about the form of Stephen Staunton – and who would have guessed that before we left Ireland. Throughout the preliminary rounds of the competition, he's been our best player, a superb rallying point on those occasions when we found ourselves under the cosh.

But Stephen has suffered more than most here because of his blond hair and fair complexion. It was no surprise that he was one of the players who insisted on wearing a cap before the Italian match, yet in spite of all the precautions and his fierce commitment, he didn't perform to pedigree.

That has implanted a few doubts in my mind and caused me to look at all my options. But having balanced it out, I think I'm justified in keeping him in the side in the hope that it will come right for him tomorrow.

Normally, the day before a game is relatively quiet in the afternoon, but not this one. It's now 8.45 p.m. and I'm still in the gear in which I left the training ground this morning. Put that down to four television interviews, as many more with the written press, and watching two reruns of football videos. I tell you something. This job doesn't get any easier with experience.

24 · June · 1994

There is this huge window in my suite, all of ten feet deep, and it's a pain in the neck to find the right strings to draw the different curtains in the morning. And I'm lying there in the bed, half-afraid to open them for fear of what I might see.

Secretly, I'm hoping it's bucketing down outside or, at worst, cloudy. And if I'm lucky, there may just be a bit of a breeze. But I don't want to get up to find out.

This is ridiculous! I haul myself out of bed and in a flamboyant gesture pull them wide open. And my heart sinks. For out there as far as the eye can see is blue sky with not a trace of cloud in sight. There and then I know it's going to be a scorcher of a day – just the kind we've been dreading.

Because it's a noon kick-off, we have to be on the coach taking us to the game by ten o'clock. Now normally, as you will be aware by now, we go for a little stroll in the grounds of our hotel on match day, but not this time. It's just too warm to move, and even leaving the air conditioning of the hotel to walk to the coach is a jolt to the senses.

There is also air conditioning in the dressing room and that's a blessed relief. But with the exception of Packie Bonner and Alan Kelly, there will be no warm up exercises on the pitch for anybody. We'll just walk out for two minutes, look at the crowd, get the feel of the place and head back inside.

Once in there, we stock up on liquids containing salt, sugar, iron, and all the things we will lose in fluid during the next ninety minutes or so. For the last three weeks we've trained specifically for this day, and now we're going to find out if it's been long enough and hard enough to sustain us in our hour of need.

Giants Stadium was warm, but really it is the Mexican game which has been on my mind from day one. And it doesn't do our morale any good to be told that the temperature in the stadium is 110 degrees. When we walk out alongside the Mexicans I say to myself: 'How in the name of God are we going to handle this?'

In fact, we handle it quite well for 35 or 40 minutes. We're putting some good moves together, getting in behind their defence now and then and generally closing them down effectively in midfield.

With any luck, we should have been ahead inside ten minutes when Terry Phelan and Roy Keane split the cover down the left. As the cross skids along the six yard area, Tommy Coyne is only a split second late in making the vital contact in front of an open goal.

Later still, Roy sets up a chance for Andy Townsend, but the header is collected by the Mexican goalkeeper, Campos, just inside the post. Taken in conjunction with the first miss, this is disappointing, but still I'm pretty happy with the way the first quarter has gone.

The down side is a yellow card for Dennis Irwin for delaying throwing in the ball, and with a card already standing against him from the Italian match, that means he's out of the game against Norway next Tuesday. That, in my opinion, is a very harsh decision, for there was no question of Dennis deliberately wasting time – not at this stage in the match. We'd only been playing twenty minutes and we were on top at that stage.

So much for FIFA's earlier edict that there would be sufficient stoppages and the game would be slowed down sufficiently to enable players to come to the side-lines to get water. Incredibly, the linesman, for all the controversy of the last fortnight, is still refusing to allow us to throw bags on to the pitch.

I call the fourth FIFA match official, who is also the reserve referee, and complain. In fairness, he instructs the linesman that he's mistaken, that it is in fact permissible to throw in the water bags.

As in the Italian match, the wide players are getting plenty of liquids. Everytime we give them a bag, they take a sip, pour the rest over their heads and chuck them back. And I roar: 'Don't be so bloody selfish. What about the players inside you? Let them have a drink too.' But in the din of the place, they obviously don't hear me, and people like Paul, Phil, Andy, Roy and Tommy are again the victims.

Then, approaching half-time, there is an

 Everyone suffered in the heat of Orlando against Mexico. Here Roy Keane gets some much needed water.

Terry Phelan and Dennis Irwin sum up our day against Mexico (above) while I walk off at the end.

ominous development. The gap between our midfielders and the back four is getting progressively wider. We're not sharp enough in closing them down and I turn to Maurice and say: 'We're in trouble. The lads are tiring. The heat is getting to them.'

Still, there are only three minutes to the break and I'm looking forward to getting them into the dressing room and some liquid down them, when suddenly it happens. A ball bounces awkwardly for Phil Babb; he does well to get it and he's coming away with it when he's tackled sideways.

In quicker time than it takes to tell, it runs loose to a Mexican, is knocked in, then back out to Luis Garcia, and from twenty yards, he slots it in just by Packie's right-hand post. One down. I protest: 'But we should have closed the boy down.' But when I look at the tired faces out there in front of me, can I really blame them?

It took us some time to recover our composure in the second half and during that period the Mexicans have a couple of good chances. But we have one too, when the ball is played through to John Sheridan with the goalkeeper some yards off his line. But John has to take it early, and in attempting to chip Campos, he gets it wrong and we live to rue the miss.

And we're still in there with a chance of a point when Dennis Irwin, of all people, blows it. The ball is played down the left and Dennis, fatally, lets it bounce. I'm standing there yelling at him when a Mexican takes it off him, comes inside, checks and heads for the penalty area. And worse still, Paul McGrath is positioned yards away from him.

As soon as the Mexican checked his cross-field run and turned into the penalty area, Paul should have nailed him there and then. But he's nowhere near him, and just as he had done in

the first half, Luis Garcia squeezes the ball in off the bottom of the post and we're now two down.

On another day and in a different match, it might have struck either the outside or middle of the post and rebounded back into play. But this is our luck on the day and we must grin and bear it.

In fact, I've already stripped Alan Kernaghan and was getting ready to substitute Paul when our world fell apart for a second time. A few minutes earlier I had noticed Paul bending over with his arms across his chest, trying to get his breath, and decided that he was in real trouble.

Having gone two goals down, if we're going to get anything out of the game, I need two pairs of fresh legs. So McGrath stays and I decide to bring on Jason McAteer and John Aldridge in place of Stephen Staunton and Tommy Coyne.

Stephen hasn't played at any time like the way he can play. The heat is just too much for him and Tommy has given his all. At this point he can only get weaker, so I haul him off.

I give Charlie O'Leary the names of the two substitutes and he goes and hands them to the fourth FIFA official. All the while, I'm roaring instructions to the lads on the pitch, telling Ray to come over to the left side and advising Roy Keane to push a little more forward.

As I'm looking for Aldo on the pitch, I can't find him. Jason is in the game all right. I'd actually brought Aldo up to the ref to push him on but now I notice that he's still standing there on the touchline, fuming because a guy in a blue hat and a yellow coat refuses to let him on.

I say to Charlie: 'What the hell is going on?' Charlie tells me that the FIFA guy won't allow John on. Then I notice that this fellow still has the slip of paper in his hand. So I say to him: 'What are you doing with that? The referee should have that paper.'

And he roars at me: 'You get back. You don't know, it's none of your business', and he starts pushing me. I say: 'Pal, you're out of order.' Then I notice that I've stepped over the line and promptly retreat.

Anyway, Aldo eventually gets on after all the confusion. Then Jason does precisely what he was meant to do, and with seven minutes to go, he measures the cross which Aldo puts away with his head. Suddenly, a glimmer of hope opens up on this dreadful day.

In fact, we're now running stronger than the opposition, getting at them down both wings, and I sense there is just a chance that we'll plunder an equaliser. Sadly, that fond hope goes out the window when Campos pulls off a flying save from Andy and I know we're beaten.

The dressing room, as you can imagine, is quiet and sullen. I go to do my press conference and the only people there seem to be Mexican journalists. They keep asking me to confirm that their team is brilliant. I tell them they've some very good players, and I like the way they play, but if they come and play us in our kinds of conditions, they'll get a different result. They don't want to hear that, so I leave.

On the coach ride back to the hotel, Andy Townsend comes and tells me that the players have had a meeting and they don't wish to go to Disneyland as arranged tomorrow. So I gather them around and tell them that I've made an honest mistake – I didn't realise that the third game against Norway was coming up so quickly, in just four days' time.

It means that we have only a couple of days to recover our strength, and with the trip back to New York on Sunday going to eat up most of that day, we're running short of time.

I'd now prefer if they didn't go walking around in the sun tomorrow, but I've made them a promise and if they wish, I'll keep it. And if it helps them to water down the disappointment for their wives and children, they can blame me.

That suits fine and agreement is reached before we arrive back in the hotel. There will be no wild living tonight, only a few quiet drinks and doubtless long, painful inquests into how the game got away from us.

25 · June · 1994

We do the grandparents' thing this morning as Pat and I go shopping at the local mall for presents for the children back home. We arrive back in the team hotel in the early afternoon and there are loads of journalists hanging about the place. Something is stirring.

Sure enough, I've just stepped into the lobby when these two newsmen come over and tell that I'm in trouble. They inform me that FIFA have banned me from the bench for one game and fined me 20,000 Swiss francs which, I soon discover, amounts to £7,000. Additionally, John Aldridge has been fined for his part in the incident. And my first question is – what incident?

They can't tell me and since the FAI delegation is on a day's outing to Disneyland, I'm left totally in the dark. The only thing I can think of is that confrontation with the FIFA guy over John Aldridge's substitution but surely that can't be the reason.

And all the while, the journalists are buzzing about, wanting me to say something provocative. But, in this instance at least, I'm honestly unaware of any offence I've committed. I ask the guy on the reception desk at the hotel if there have been any fax messages for me and he says no. If I'm being banned, wouldn't you think they'd have the courtesy to give me a reason?

Then Michael Hyland and Sean Connolly come into the hotel and they confirm that a statement had been issued in Dallas at four o'clock that afternoon and that I have, in fact, been disciplined. But they, like me, are in the dark about the alleged crime.

A BBC man comes up and tells me that they've just put together a sequence on film of the bits in which I was involved and would I care to see them. Of course I would, and they confirm my belief that I am totally innocent. They show the altercation from three different angles and it proves that while the original dispute is going on, I've stood yelling instructions at players on the pitch.

It does prove, however, that the person causing all the fuss is the blue-coated FIFA official who at the end of the sequence appears to go berserk about me.

Now, all the evidence is that John Aldridge was guilty because he swore at the official. He said something like – 'You're a bloody cheat.'

The reason was that he'd just been pulled unfairly off the park by this Egyptian guy.

Other than that, however, nothing happened. In fact, the only mistake made was that by the Egyptian in refusing or omitting to hand to the referee the slip of paper with the name of the substitution. I didn't abuse anybody and I defy anybody to prove otherwise.

Some people come to me later and say that this is FIFA's way of getting back at me for criticising them, first on Dr Havelange's statement on referees and second on the water bag issue. Or maybe it's because we were cautioned at one point by the linesman about the lads on the bench standing up on occasions to follow play.

But all teams do that when play is in the corner of the pitch – it's human nature. Surely that's not a cause of a fine like this?

And already, there are stories going out in the papers which have me swearing at the referee and insulting people generally. Rubbish! I can say that during the Mexican game I never approached any of the three match officials.

The exception was early in the game when a linesman told us that we were not allowed to throw on water bags and he was promptly corrected by the fourth official standing alongside me. Other than that, I had no contact with any of the three.

26 · June · 1994

Yesterday's events are still bothering me, and to make things worse there's a delay of two hours or more on the plane taking us to New York for the game against Norway on Tuesday.

When we get there, I discover that there is a battery of photographers waiting for me. Bloody hell! I've just been suspended for a game and fined, but surely that's not such a big story. But in the way of the media, I am suddenly the

 Gary Kelly got better and better as the finals went on. He's one of our rising stars.

newsmaker, the villain of the piece.

And of course they expect me to smile. But I don't feel like smiling. I've just been condemned for something I didn't do, with no right of appeal and apparently no way of making my point. And these people still want me to smile?

But I hold my temper, get on the coach taking us to the hotel, and there discover that the same guys who were on the tarmac at the airport have now rushed back and are there to hassle us again at the hotel. There must be thirty or forty photographers and camera crews lined across the entrance and there's no way through.

This time I flip. There's this guy standing inside the hotel and he pushes his camera into my face. I warn him that if he does it again, I'll take action; when he ignores me I put my hand up and push him and his camera to one side.

And I'm swearing at him and that annoys me still more. I shouldn't be swearing because that's all the guy wants – a story that will be flashed on all the news bulletins that evening. Come on Jack, handle it with a bit of humour! At this precise moment, I don't feel like being humorous. But, if I'm a professional, I can't allow them to come between me and my job. So, I start to smile again and perhaps that pleases them.

In the evening, there is another meeting with FAI officials over the fine. They interview Charlie O'Leary and myself about the events leading up to the substitutions and they, like us, are agreed that no offence has taken place. In conversation with the senior medical officer, Martin Walsh, the previous evening, he suggested that the proper course of action was to write back to FIFA asking for clarification of the charges levelled against me.

If I was in the dark about any transgression of rules – and I genuinely was – they were duty bound to specify the offence. Otherwise, there was a real risk that I would break them again. Martin felt that if we wrote to them, they would be obliged to reply. I wonder.

27 · June · 1994

Sean Connolly informs me that pub collections have begun back in Ireland to meet the cost of the fines and that already they've raised more than £10,000. That's a reassuring gesture by the Irish public but if there's a fine to be paid, I'll pay it myself – I can afford it. I suggest, however, that we sit on it for the time being and when the fund has reached a certain point, we'll give it to charity.

Today's training schedule is light, for while the forecast is for a drop in temperature in New Jersey tomorrow, the lads must be given an opportunity of relaxing and getting some strength back into their bodies.

Moreover, I've got a couple of difficult team choices to make, and irrespective of what the Norwegian camp does, I will not be making a team announcement until the very last minute.

For one thing, I've got to replace my two full-backs, Dennis Irwin and Terry Phelan, both of whom are suspended. Dennis, I thought, was very unfortunate to pick up a second yellow card. Fair enough, he was late in the tackle for the first offence against Italy but to accuse him of wasting time with the throw-in so early in the Mexican game was plain stupid.

Terry, on the other hand, was just silly and I've had a bit of a go at him over that card against Mexico. I'm sure he had no intention of hurting the Mexican player, but that kind of threatening attitude ought to have no place in a game, particularly at a time when referees are only looking for an excuse to exercise their authority.

Still, the full-back positions are no real problem. As I said, I was in two minds about whether to start with Irwin or Gary Kelly in the first place. Dennis is an exceptionally good player but I've got to take account of the fact that Gary has handled the heat better than anybody here.

And at left back, I'll almost certainly go with Stephen Staunton. If young Kelly has coped best of all in these conditions, Stephen is at the other end of the scale. In this kind of heat, he just doesn't have the legs to do a midfield job for me.

So, I'll put him in his old position at left back and bring in Jason McAteer on the right side of midfield with Raymond swapping wings. I think it's time Jason got settled into the team. He's an excellent runner with the ball and moreover he produces the crosses which get results.

That's the easy part. But what do I do about the 'hole' in midfield and, even more critically, how do I react to Paul McGrath's problems in central defence?

I've been thinking about playing Ronnie Whelan these last few days for he's looked as sharp as he's ever been in training. And in a situation in which we need experience, he could be just the man we need.

On balance, however, I think I'll push Roy Keane forward and ask John Sheridan to play in front of the back four. Roy is good at getting into the box whereas John is more of a support player. And I've got to remember that Sheridan has run bloody hard in our last two games.

But what about Paul? I've had a word with him in training this morning and told him straight up that I was disappointed with his performance against Mexico. He appeared to be knackered long before the others and I told him that he should have been on to the Mexican long before he put the ball away for the second goal.

He accepted the criticism but reminded me that he wasn't the only one who felt knackered in the heat. Clearly, however, the man is struggling with his injuries and he's honest enough to admit it.

He tells me that he can't use his arm as leverage when jumping for the ball and that unbalances him. It means that he can't head the ball properly, which worries me. Tomorrow's game will be a lot more physical than the one against Mexico and the certainty is that the Norwegians will be throwing a lot of high balls into our box. In that situation, can I honestly afford to gamble on Paul in his present condition? I tell him I'm thinking of dropping him and he tells me that he desperately wants to play.

I have a word with Andy Townsend about him and he advises that I stay with McGrath. He's like this all the time at Villa, he says, a waste of time in training but deadly effective on match days.

I also consult Kevin Moran, who rooms with Paul, and I tell him that I'm thinking of resting McGrath and bringing in Alan Kernaghan. And Kevin's first words are, 'What about me?'

So I have to be brutally honest and remind Kevin that because of his injury problems, he's missed almost all the heat training and while he's now doing the work, I don't regard him as ready for this particular game. If only as an exercise for next season's European championship, I reckon I should go with a partnership of Kernaghan and Phil Babb.

Kevin disagrees. This is a one-off match, he says, and the best players on the day should play. So I tell him that in the circumstances I regard Alan as the best on the day and, reluctantly perhaps, he takes the point.

It's a very difficult situation all round. At this point, however, I believe Kernaghan and Babb are the men to do the business for me tomorrow.

28 · June · 1994

The first item on my agenda is to have a word with Paul McGrath – and I've good news for him. I tell him I'm going to take a chance with him; and clearly he is relieved to know that he will, after all, have the chance of putting the nightmare of the Mexican game behind him.

It has not been an easy decision to make. Going to bed last night I was still thinking in terms of Alan Kernaghan, wondering how he might handle the aerial battery which I fully expect the Norwegians to launch.

But after turning it over in my mind a dozen times, I'm going to go with what I know. I agree with Andy Townsend that the psychology bit works with Paul: when you spell it out for him, he'll put his mind to it and get the job done.

Besides, I'm already committed to replacing my two full backs. To make a third change in defence might be stretching things too far. More than that, I think young Gary Kelly is capable of extracting a bit of pace from Paul whereas it may be different with Alan.

Up front, I decide to go with John Aldridge and to give Tommy Coyne a little rest. Tommy has run his guts out in two games and Aldo, I figure, will be in just the right mood to do some

damage after that spectacular late goal against Mexico.

The mood in the coach as we set off for the Giants Stadium is sombre. We all expected that ours would be one of the toughest groups of the lot in the first phase of the competition, but to arrive at a situation in which all four teams are locked together on the same points mark, with similar goals difference, is something else. It means that there is absolutely no margin for error today. Whatever else, we simply cannot afford to over-commit ourselves and present the opposition with the chance of doing what they do best – hitting on the break.

The big plus, of course, is that we have an extra goal in the bank going into the match. A point will do us, whereas the Norwegians must win to qualify for the last sixteen. Then I start worrying that psychologically it might work against us. This football is a complex business.

Today is going to be something different for me. Because of the ban, it means that I cannot stand on the line. Instead, I have arranged to watch the game from one of the television commentary points and I wonder how that's going to affect my feelings.

Maurice Setters will now be in charge down

on the bench, and while I will be in contact with him by phone, it's not quite the same thing as barking out the orders personally. But at least I have the opportunity of talking with the players before they go out, and then I'm off to my perch in the stand.

As it works out, there is a lot less hassle than I had imagined. Our plan is to play it tight at the back, keep our shape in midfield and never at any stage send more than one midfielder into the box to work alongside Aldo. And we do it perfectly.

Norway, as is their style, position their midfield players just in front of their back four. Because of the situation in which they now find themselves, I'm expecting them to push forward a little more but, incredibly, they're still playing it as conservatively as ever.

Obviously, they are still gambling on us over-committing ourselves and then hitting us with the long ball aimed at Justein Flo. But Flo is getting no change at all from Stephen Staunton, who, in a situation in which he is not required to run for 90 minutes, is looking more like his old self at left back.

By half-time neither side has created a chance of note but that suits me fine. I get down to the dressing room at the break and I preach again the gospel of vigilance and avoiding unnecessary risks.

Even if the Norwegians, by some chance, score, I believe we are capable of getting back at them. But that's a situation I don't wish to face unless we have to, and the way things are going I don't see it happening.

For the second half, Norway choose to use Flo down the left wing but he gets as little change out of Gary Kelly as he did from Stephen. For a small lad, Gary gets up surprisingly high and it's amazing how he's handling a big six-footer like Flo.

The Norwegians have a good spell at the start of the second half and for one unnerving moment they look like scoring. There is an inswinging corner on our left and instead of coming forward, Packie goes backwards. And the next thing the ball is bobbing around in our six-yard area before somebody knocks it just over the top. Bloody hell! Norway haven't looked like scoring since the game started and yet here we are almost a goal down because of a silly mistake.

That, I can assure you, doesn't do anything for the blood pressure but then young Jason starts to run at them a bit more and suddenly we're out of our crisis. The game is being played more and more away from our posts and that has to be a tribute to the way people like Roy Keane in particular are grafting in midfield.

And then John Sheridan has a chance of wrapping it up for us, but his neat little chip, which I suspect will be replayed many times on television, just goes over. I could have done with that going in but I'm still confident we can get the result we need.

In the last quarter, I bring on Ronnie Whelan and David Kelly to give us extra running power and Ronnie, in fact, almost gets in for the winner. But with the Norwegian cover broken, he is just pipped in a race to the ball with the goalkeeper.

And all the time, I'm listening in for news of Italy's game with Mexico which is being played at precisely the same time. That's one advantage of sitting with the television people. The news I'm getting suggests that the other match is as tight as ours. The teams are drawing 1-1, and if the scorelines in the two matches stay as they are, that means the Norwegians are out.

 Houghton and Flo together (top) and Bratseth and Aldridge (below) in the final qualifying match against Norway.

That's me with the fans before the Norway match. I went there again when it was all over, to share in the celebrations.

Presumably, Egil Olsen, the Norwegian manager, is also aware of what is happening but if it induces extra urgency from them, it is not immediately apparent. Or perhaps that's the measure of the way our lads have gone about their job professionally and carried out their instructions to the letter.

We're sitting on them in midfield and, unlike their earlier two games, they're not getting the time to throw the ball into our penalty area. It's all going to plan from our point of view and then, suddenly, the referee spreads his arms and it's all over.

We've got the point we needed and now we're on our way to the knock-out stages of the championship. The first objective of our stay in America has been achieved and I'm naturally delighted.

Back in the dressing room, there is an unmistakable feeling of a job well done and I congratulate each of the players individually. Then Sean Connolly comes in and tells me that the Irish supporters are still out in the stadium, waiting for me to come out and give them a wave.

And when I go out, there is this wonderful reception which I'll never forget. They give me a massive cheer and I feel both privileged and grateful. Most of them have been on the road with us, all over Europe, for the last two years,

and I am thrilled to be able to give them the result they wanted.

Afterwards, the scenes in the stadium are chaotic. We're supposed to meet up with our wives in the stand but it takes us the best part of half an hour to find them. And all the time people are thumping me on the back and – would you believe it – hurting me.

So I pluck this lad from the crowd, hit him on the back and say, 'Now that's what it bloody feels like for me.' And he thinks I'm crackers. And I tell him I'm only kidding – I just want this lot to stop hitting me.

Things are not much quieter back in the hotel. The place is over-run with fans and every time I try to get to the bar for a drink, they're coming over looking for pictures or autographs.

Now, I'm the first to acknowledge what our supporters have done for us. But I just wish some of them would realise that there are times when we all like to be left alone to have a drink with our families and friends. As it is, I'm finding myself confined to my room more and more any time I want to socialise.

Tonight things are particularly bad. Three times I leave my room to go and have a drink at the bar and three times I have to retreat. Would you believe, it is 1.30 in the morning before the place quietens sufficiently for me to go down and have a beer or two with Trevor O'Rourke.

29 · June · 1994

A free day for the players but not, alas, for the manager. While the rest of the lads prepare to go out with their families, I'm up at the crack of dawn to catch a flight from Newark airport to Washington to watch Belgium in action against Saudi Arabia.

Depending on the other results, we may be meeting one of these teams in the next round, and while I've seen both play on television, I want to have another look at them and check out key players and their style of play.

As it happens, it's a fruitless journey – and one which I won't forget for a long time. For a start, thunderstorms on the east coast delay our departure and instead of arriving in Washington at 10 a.m., we get to the stadium just as the players are coming out on the park.

I'm with an RTE television crew and they, like me, can only have been amazed by the way the game went. The critics had the Belgians as favourites to win it and sure enough for most of the ninety minutes they were all over the Saudis. Their finishing was so bad, however, that at times it was embarrassing. Instead of winning handsomely, they end up losing 1-0.

We're still talking about the Saudi's good fortune when the results of the other games begin to filter through and I discover to my annoyance that I've wasted my time coming here. It emerges that we will now be meeting Holland for a place in the quarter-finals and, here's the rub, we must go back to Orlando to play it.

Damn it all, I thought we had finished with that place. The only consolation on this occasion is that we'll be playing another European team. Unlike the Mexicans, they won't be able to run all day in that heat and humidity.

After a meal with George Hamilton and the rest of the RTE lads, we go our separate ways and then things really start going wrong. I've met up with an old friend from Skipton, Dave Hickson, who takes me out to the airport; when we get there we discover there is a lot of traffic congestion.

The electrical storms which have been raging in the area at different times of the day are still causing problems and as we sit on the plane waiting for the weather to improve, the captain comes on and tell us that if we don't get out before ten o'clock, we're stuck in Washington for the rest of the night. Apparently, the plane is too big and too powerful to conform to the noise restrictions in the vicinity of the airport after ten o'clock.

It's now past 9.30 p.m. and yes, the next announcement on the tannoy is that the flight has been cancelled and we're all off the plane. That, I discover, is only the start of my problems. All flights to Orlando the following day are fully booked up and they can't get me a hotel room in Washington.

Hell's gates! I tell them I'm the manager of a team still involved in the World Cup and I just have to be in Orlando the following day. So the guy goes back to his computer and tells me that there is a small plane leaving for Atlanta around midnight and that I can get a connection there for a flight to Florida at seven o'clock the next morning.

In my desperation, I take it, and so begins one of the most uncomfortable nights of my entire life. We're stuck in bloody Atlanta airport for the night and believe me, it's not a pretty experience. Dave Hickson lies on the floor and I try to make myself comfortable on a hard plastic seat but neither of us can afford to close an eye for fear somebody will pinch our bags. And back home, people are thinking what a great life these football managers have!

 Packie Bonner holds his head after letting in that goal against Holland.

*E*ventually I get to the team hotel around ten o'clock this morning and I make my plans clear. I'm off to bed and I don't want anybody to disturb me until at least 4 p.m.

Today is a write off. I'm still sound asleep when I get my prearranged phone call at 5 p.m. – and I'm immediately into hassle. It appears that there was a bit of a tiff on the coach taking the squad back to the hotel from the Giants Stadium when Mick Byrne attempted unsuccessfully to get his son and daughter-in-law a lift on the bus.

I'm unaware of this dispute which essentially concerns Mick and Joe Delaney until I awaken this afternoon and learn that Mick is refusing to leave his room and threatening to go home. So I go down and have a word with him and he repeats the threat that he is going back to Dublin as a mark of protest about the way his son was treated. And my first reaction is to see red – with Mick! I tell him that I've been up the whole bloody night and the last thing I want to be confronted with is threats. And I tell him that if that's the way he feels, he should pack his bags and go.

And immediately I've said it, I'm sorry. Mick is enormously popular with the lads because he's prepared to work twelve or fourteen hours a day with them. The man hasn't had a day off in five weeks, and if he feels like blowing his top, the least I should do is listen to him. So I do.

Joe Delaney is also under strain for, like Mick, he's been working all hours of the day for the common good. I put the dispute down to stress and tell him that if anything like this should arise again, I'll deal with it directly.

With the air finally cleared, Mick Byrne is soon about his job again. And inevitably, most of his time is given over to Paul McGrath. Although Paul stepped up a lot on his performance against Mexico, he is still not fit by accepted international standards.

Apart from his knee problems, his shoulder is still troubling him – and clearly it's not going to get any better for the remainder of our time here. Taking everything into consideration he's done brilliantly, but I need him to be in as good a shape as possible for the Dutch game.

Andy Townsend's knee still needs looking at, for while he discharged his primary responsibilities well on Tuesday, he wasn't the player he can be. More than ever, we need him to be fit and at the top of his form to give us a solid midfield base against Holland.

Young Roy is flying, and when you think of the amount of grafting he did in the game, that's amazing. The lad's engine is incredible.

I'm still a bit concerned about Big Cas. He's beginning to do a little more work now but that leg of his looks far from sound and we're beginning to run out of time in the attempt to get it right. I feel sorry for the lad. He's had a terrible season with injuries, and after getting the push at Chelsea, he needs to do well out here to put himself on show for potential buyers.

We need him, too. In contrast to our strategy throughout the qualifying games, we've been forced to play here without a big man up front. Cas at his best is capable of doing a lot of damage to opposing defences, but looking at him now he's not nearly ready to get through the full ninety minutes of a game.

This effectively will be our last brisk training session before we meet the Dutch and we'll make the best of it.

The usual rules apply: people with any kind of knocks don't train. With the heat work long since done, the sessions are not nearly as tough on the players now as they were back in the first week of our stay here but it's very important to keep them on the boil.

We stay at Seminole for lunch and then early in the afternoon the heavens open and I'm glad that we have no further work planned for that day. The lads have the option of going out for a couple of hours or so, but most of them decline and stay in the hotel.

The word I'm getting from Ireland is that the collection for the fine is now nearing six figures – and that staggers me. As I've said, I'll pay the fine myself, but it's very reassuring to know that there is so much good will for us back home.

Mind you I'm not so sure if the same commodity is in plentiful supply at FIFA headquarters. It's now four days since we posted off that letter asking for clarification of the offences which I am alleged to have committed, but as yet we haven't heard a word from them.

In a sense I'm not greatly surprised, but after all those fax messages which were flying around over tackles and water bags before the championship started, I thought they just might stir themselves to forward some kind of explanation.

We go to the Citrus Bowl to train this morning. I'm not sure whether it's a case of getting used to the heat or the temperature dropping, but somehow it doesn't seem quite as intimidating as before. Perhaps it's a case of knowing that this time we will not have to meet the Mexicans. The cloud ceiling is again pretty low and that's a help.

Paul McGrath is again on the easy list today but Cas does a small bit of work. The remainder of the lads seem to be fine, so it doesn't look as if there will be many fitness problems to complicate the team selection.

I'm getting different reports from the Dutch camp. Some suggest that Dick Advocaat, their manager, is going to stay with what he knows best and name all the established players in his team.

Others suggest that after the lessons of Tilburg and our 1-0 win there, he's going to ring the changes and dispense with some of the older players. I am not, of course, privy to the happenings in the Dutch camp but I'll be greatly surprised if the second supposition turns out to be true.

I just cannot see Advocaat changing tack at this stage of the competition. He will, of course, have that Tilburg game at the back of his mind but I'll be amazed if he allows it to cloud his thoughts to the point where he's ready to sacrifice experience.

Players like Ronald Koeman, Frank Reykaard, William Jonk and Dennis Bergkamp are all central to his strategy. There is simply no way, in my opinion, that he can afford to go without them.

In the afternoon, we watch a video of the Switzerland-Spain game and later tune in to Germany and Belgium. Slowly but surely, the championship is taking shape. The Spaniards win with some style against the Swiss, proving that when they get it together they can be very impressive. Germany win the other game and, given the history of recent World Cup championships, that can have surprised few.

3 · July · 1994

It's another overcast morning. I'm ready to believe now that conditions in the Citrus Bowl tomorrow will be tolerable but that statement is, of course, relative. Even on the most favourable day the place is intimidating for any European team, and the best we can hope for is that the heat and humidity won't be too bad.

All my thoughts today are dominated by the team selection and the side I'll send out tomorrow. I hear that the Dutch are not going to name their selection until tomorrow, but even if they choose today I'll be taking advantage of that sixty-minute option and waiting until the very last minute.

The reasoning behind that is that I wish to wait to see what kind of a day it will be and if it is likely to suit Stephen Staunton in particular. It's now accepted by everybody that Stephen has not had a good tournament to date and that, of course, is down to his fair complexion and his inability to cope with the heat.

In normal conditions, he could have been one of the players of the championship but now his performances have dropped to a level where I am giving serious thought to the possibility of leaving him out.

Nobody has to remind me what we owe Stephen for getting this far. But we simply cannot afford to carry passengers. If it's a warm day tomorrow, I'm afraid he's out. Otherwise I'm prepared to take a chance.

Up front, I have three options: Tommy Coyne, John Aldridge and David Kelly. Aldo, of course, is the most experienced of the trio, and looking at him in training I can sense how desperately anxious he is to play. But at this point I'm inclining towards Tommy. He's had a good rest now since his last game against Mexico, and with his enormous workrate I reckon he's the man for this particular job.

Without doubt, however, the greatest dilemma of all is whether to play Dennis Irwin or Gary Kelly at right back. To drop a player like Dennis Irwin is, in many ways, unthinkable. He's been a tremendous full back for us, always dependable, always guaranteed to turn it on when we need him.

But how do I leave out young Kelly? He's been flying ever since we got here and my mind keeps going back to that game in Tilburg when he didn't give the boy Roy a kick of the ball. Now, I've no way of knowing if Roy will be in the Dutch side this time, but even so I'm inclining towards Gary.

I'll have another think about it tomorrow morning and hopefully I'll get it right. Meanwhile, we're off to the television room to have a look at the video of Holland's game against Belgium.

It's all over. We're out of the World Cup after the defeat by Holland. Andy Townsend turns to salute the best fans in the world.

Back home
in Dublin. At
the airport
(left) and at
the Lark in
the Park
(below).

I'm peeping out the window again this morning and this time I like what I see. There is a lot of cloud about and while this does not necessarily mean a mild day, the temperature certainly won't get into three figures. And when you play in Orlando, that's a relief.

We do the usual things including our little walk, and before we get on the coach I give the lads the team. And, after all the agonising, I have to tell Dennis Irwin that I'm leaving him out and playing Gary Kelly at right back.

That, for me, was one of the hardest decisions I've had to make as Ireland team manager and it must have been harder for Dennis. I take him aside and explain the situation to him and to his great credit he takes it very well. Dennis is that kind of lad.

I'm also going to play Stephen Staunton, and that has as much to do with the weather as anything else. Tommy Coyne will play up front, and after giving some thought to playing Jason McAteer on the right side of midfield, I've decided to stay with Raymond.

He's not the best finisher in the world but he's had a good World Cup so far and I'm impressed by his workrate. I know he'll give me another 100 per cent effort today, and if he tires I can always revert to plan B.

Before we leave the hotel, I check again on our travel and accommodation plans for the quarter-finals. If we beat the Dutch, we meet either Brazil or the United States who are playing this afternoon. Irrespective of who wins that game, we're headed for Dallas next Saturday if we qualify, and Joe Delaney and Eddie Corcoran have gone there just to check out the accommodation.

Travelling to the Citrus Bowl, we notice that there are as many Irish supporters as ever here. The word we had was that some of those who attended the first phase games had returned home, but if they did there were loads of replacements.

There are also a lot of Dutch fans making their way to the ground and it makes for a great splash of green and orange. Whatever else, this game is not going to lack atmosphere.

Once at the stadium, we do the usual things. The warm-up exercises will again be undertaken indoors for while it's not nearly as hot or humid as before, I don't want the lads out on the pitch too long before it starts.

I also check out the water arrangements and those for making substitutions. I'm still in the dark as to what I did wrong the last time I was here but it seems that unless you ask and ask you don't get any information.

We go over our match plan again, stress the things we must and must not do and then – it's kick-off time. We start quite well, get at their back four once or twice, and after five minutes or so we almost score.

The referee gives us a free kick just outside the box and Stephen goes for power. Unfortunately, it strikes a defender on his knee and in a situation in which it might have gone anywhere, the ball flies over the crossbar.

To their credit, the Dutch are also ready to have a go and they seem to be directing their attacks down the left to test out young Gary. Twice they get in behind him and we all go, 'bloody hell'! Already, it's obvious that they've absorbed the lessons of the Tilburg game and are determined to give us some of our own medicine.

They're getting balls in behind us, and any time we try to get out at them, they push us back in. This is not like the Dutch and it's causing us problems.

And it's in that kind of situation that they break us for the first vital goal. A ball is knocked in behind Terry Phelan, but with the nearest Dutch player eight or ten yards away from him, there's no real danger. Terry has plenty of time and room to do what he likes with it, either knock it back to Packie or across to Phil Babb who's standing square with him.

But the fact that nobody is pressurising him is fatal for our Terry. In the normal course of events he would have knocked it back or hoofed it clear, but here he allows the ball to bounce a second time and instinctively the Dutch lad, who by now senses that something may be on for him, starts chasing.

After what seems like an eternity, Phelan goes to head the ball back to the keeper, but he allows it come down too far before doing so and there's nowhere near enough power on the ball to carry through to Packie. And in that split second I know we are doomed.

The Dutch player takes it to the back line, crosses, and Bergkamp, like the good striker he is, pulls away just enough to side-foot it in at the near post. One-nil and I bloody cringe at the thought of it. Of all the stupid goals, of all the silly things for Terry to go and do – this takes the biscuit.

Now it's a real mountain-climbing job for us but we respond well. Andy and Roy are getting stuck in at midfield and more and more the ball is travelling in the direction of Holland's posts. We have one or two half-chances over the next ten or fifteen minutes and one of them, inevitably, falls to Raymond. Andy puts in the cross from the left but it whistles across the goal in front of Houghton when a better finisher might have got a touch on it.

In terms of build-up and approach play, we're doing quite well but our finishing is absolutely terrible. Even in situations in which we have a little time and space, we're still messing it up.

I turn to Maurice or Mick and enquire how long there is to go to half-time and am told three minutes. And then I look back to see the big lad, Jonk, running at John Sheridan. He just dips his shoulder and he's passed John as if he just didn't exist.

Now he's running directly at the heart of our defence but he's still a good 35 yards out when he goes for the shot. In a split-second reaction, I'm happy about that for surely he'll never score from that range. It's not a particularly powerful shot and Packie has time to pick the right position and get behind the flight of the ball.

He's so well positioned that if he didn't put his hands up for it, the ball would have struck him anyway. But as he sticks up his hands it appears to catch him on the top of his fingers, just enough to take the sting out of the shot but, alas, not enough to prevent it coming down and trickling over the line.

It's the silliest goal I've seen in a long time, one that they'll be replaying on television for years and years to come and it's gone and driven a dagger through our hearts. Apart from those two crazy errors, we haven't done a thing wrong in the first half and yet we're two bloody goals down.

We come in at half-time and I mean, damn it, what do I say? I can't go shouting at either Terry or Packie for, more than anybody, they realise what they've just gone and done. So I say, 'Listen. Forget about what's happened, let's go back out there and play as we know we can play. As long as it's only 2-0, we're still in with a shout, so keep your shape, keep plugging away and hopefully we'll get a goal back. Then, we'll bloody well see how good these Dutch guys are.'

It's a pretty grim situation all round for us but what do you say in that kind of scenario at this particular stage of a World Cup?

I can't afford to make changes – at least not for some time. I can use only two subs and if I need to send on Cas to try and turn things around, it can only be for the last ten or fifteen minutes. In his present condition, he's simply not capable of playing any longer.

I want to get Jason McAteer on but only at a stage when the Dutch are beginning to tire and he can make a real impact by running at them. At this point, however, the opposition have their tails up – it'll be some time yet before they begin to flag.

Actually, we play quite well in the second half when the Dutch are under the cosh almost all the time, but our finishing is still appalling. For a team which gets together as much as we do and which has so many good strikers from midfield, it baffles me how we can get things so wrong so often once we're in the penalty area.

Raymond has at least three good chances and squanders the bloody lot. On one occasion, Stephen lifts the ball on to his head, but from only a couple of yards out he knocks it over the top. And then, when he gets another good opportunity in the inside-left position, he wastes that too.

Andy and Roy are just brilliant and it must be breaking their hearts to find themselves in a team losing 2-0 when we're playing the opposition off the park. I bring on Cas and Jason, but for all the sweat, all the frenetic effort, nothing is falling right for us.

Eventually Paul puts one away, but the referee penalises him for lifting his boot too high and I know for sure that it's just not our day. Then the whistle goes, and for me, like so many millions of Irish people around the world, the dream has ended.

It was a game I always thought we could win but never, even in my most pessimistic moments, did I visualise the Dutch beating us by two goals. And now as I sit here, reflecting on what might have been, the thing which hurts most is that we presented them with their ticket to the quarter-finals.

Ever since we arrived here, we've done things right. We set a tough schedule in training and the lads never balked. We asked them to labour in conditions which were at times excruciating – and they were as brave as any players I've ever known.

And to reflect that it's all been in vain because of two mistakes that will haunt us for the rest of our days. Football, bloody football. I think I'll go and get myself a stiff drink!